GHOSTLY TALES AND LEGENDS

ALONG THE GRAND STRAND

OF SOUTH CAROLINA

Ghostly Tales
and Legends
along the Grand Strand
of South Carolina

Blanche W. Floyd

BANDIT
BOOKS

Winston-Salem, North Carolina

Library of Congress Control Number 2002108814

ISBN 1-878177-12-5

Bandit Books, Inc.

P.O. Box 11721

Winston-Salem, NC 27116-1721

(336) 785-7417

Distributed by John F. Blair, Publisher

(800) 222-9796

www.blairpub.com

Cover design by Holly Smith, bookskins.net

For our
grandchildren
Kevin and Brad
Jennifer and David
Christy and Paul
who love
all kinds of tales

TABLE OF CONTENTS

ACKNOWLEDGMENTS

It's time for giving thanks to the many people who helped and encouraged me along the way, dear friends whose opinions I value. Such helpfulness has made a difference.

I have always had an interest in place names and their backgrounds. I encouraged my students in the public schools to look for the story behind the name and ask lots of questions. Someone may remember or send you to another for information. Often it is a dramatic search, and ghostly tales come forth in unexpected places.

Our beautiful Carolina coastline holds a myriad of tales from the storied past. Owners of plantations and town houses chose names that were nostalgic ties with the "Old Country." A vocabulary of ghosting came to us from Africa, the Caribbean islands, Ireland, Wales, Scotland, England and France—wherever settlers came from. They passed on their stories, traditions, superstitions and names for a rich heritage.

I am indebted to the writers of articles and excerpts from books found in the *Independent Republic Quarterly*, published by the Horry County Historical Society. Family letters, diaries and newspapers highlight important events. A simple line from Little River in the 1700s, "Pirates in port," opens up a line of inquiry.

I am grateful for the support and help of family members. Without my husband's help, my books would not have been written. He is my driver, photographer, proof reader and sounding board for ideas. My thanks to him for unlimited help.

Those of us who write have a responsibility to preserve the chronology of Horry County's history and its rich heritage for future generations. Sometimes we are so busy looking ahead that we neglect past events.

Our heritage in Horry County is an unusual and important asset to our way of life, to be explored and remembered.

INTRODUCTION

A LAND OF SHADOWS AND LIGHT

Everything sparkles along the Grand Strand: the foam-flecked waves of the mighty Atlantic, the brilliant white sand of the beach, and the colorful buildings, standing like tall sentinels back of the sand dunes. Entertainment glistens with light, color, and sound.

Even so, there are shadows beneath the gaiety of a marvelous resort area. The past merges with the present, and reminders surface from time to time. Ghostly impressions remain of those who have gone before: Spanish settlers and horses in 1526, startling the native Indians and treating them cruelly; bloodthirsty pirates; shackled slaves; humble settlers, seeking a place to call home; and battles for freedom fought across the land and sea.

Down through the ages, ghostly images have lived on in the memories of kindred spirits. Tales and legends of unusual occurrences have persisted for as long as men have kept written records, and even before the first picture writings or markings. Primitive tribesmen created their own lore, assigning unexplained happenings to the shadowy spirits of the past. The telling of tales over the centuries kept the past alive.

The South seems to have a special affinity for haunting tales, in spite of its natural beauty and enviable climate. Bloody battles from the American Revolution and the Civil War left true stories of defeat and despair. Remembered darkness includes the loss of lavish lifestyle enjoyed by plantation owners, which was in itself a contradiction to life in the slave villages. That heritage of slavery, the other side of the coin of the plantation lifestyle, hovers over us like a dark cloud even a century and a half later. The Reconstruction period brought hardships to all Southerners. Many lost their right to vote, and the economic system collapsed. It is no wonder the South has never forgotten "The Wahr."

Stories of its troubled past have become basic in the history of the South, especially in older settlements where the past lingers. No child in Georgetown will ever forget that the British army and the Union army, almost a century apart, stabled their horses in the classic Prince George Winyah Episcopal Church. Succeeding generations tell the story, and remember.

In coastal lands the fog sweeps in on moisture-laden winds to create cloud banks or wavering sheets of mist that suggest the presence of ghostly beings. Many tales are associated with coastal storms or heavy fog. Strange sounds and suspicious sights, repeating over the years, reinforce the tales. Every telling adds details, and the stories grow.

Early settlers in the New World brought with them a vocabulary of "ghosting." Words like witch, spook, specter, haunt or hant, plat-eye, and old hag had special meaning for believers. From England came two names less well known: piskies (pests) and knackers (tricksters). These two terms are the originators of the familiar "trick-or-treat" custom. Children in spooky costumes parade the streets near their homes, extending their bags or baskets with the cry, "Trick or treat!" Who could resist their request? Unfortunately tricks are sometimes played, and tragic accidents do occur.

Ghosts play a part in many primitive religions and cults, among them ancestor worship and witchcraft. Nature worship celebrates the changing of the seasons. Some tribes of North American Indians practiced a "Ghost Dance," where performers wore white, flowing robes and danced on dark nights. It was an eerie sight. Kindred spirits who have experienced ghostly encounters consider the area around Georgetown, Pawleys Island, and Murrells Inlet to be one of the most haunted locations on the East Coast. Georgetown and nearby areas have the honor of being named, unofficially, "The Ghost Capital of the South."

Folklore and old wives' tales, especially among the slaves and their descendents, played an important part in the heritage of the great plantations. Many old houses in Georgetown and the manor houses on the plantations claim resident ghosts. The legends grow with each generation. Then too, someone has said that the coastal area is such a pleasant place to live that no one wants to leave. Even those who have long since departed this life keep coming back.

Fall months are great times for telling tales and legends. In October, tours in Georgetown may take you to town houses or country places, in search of ghostly sights and sounds. Dark-o'-the-moon story telling at Atalaya, the Huntington home at Huntington State Park, draws crowds of visitors. The story of Old Gunn Church, on Plantersville Road, never fails to add to the shivery excitement of young people.

The fall season, marked by changing colors and rustling leaves, seems to be a time of waiting and listening. Sometimes faint footsteps are heard where no one walks and no trail can be found. The bright harvest moon casts macabre shadows, and goblins hide behind every bush. Unexplained lights hover in the distance. Sounds of an organ and choir whisper on the breeze from an old burned-out church, long deserted. Galloping horses race down a strip of road in a forested section. A beleaguered pirate seeks refuge and a resting place in the bays near the Grand Strand. A chair rocks in an upper room of an old house, though no one is there.

From ancient lore and primitive legends comes a fearful warning, "Beware! The ghosting season is upon us!"

1

ALICE OF THE HERMITAGE

The plain marble slab, mottled and discolored after a century and a half, marks the grave of a beautiful but unhappy young girl. The only word on the slab is "Alice." No family name, or dates, or epitaph extolling her virtues or any achievements, just the simple name "Alice" identifies the grave.

An aura of mystery hangs over the site. Ancient oaks, with wisps of moss blowing in the slight breeze, line the walkways of All Saints Parish, Waccamaw Cemetery in Pawleys Island. Many people believe it is the grave of Alice Flagg, the lady in white of the Hermitage. It seems that hers is a restless spirit, still searching for her lost ring after all these years.

The trench worn around the marble slab shows how many people come, year after year, to see her grave, retell her story, place a flowery nosegay on her resting place, and peer fearfully through the trees for a glimpse of her ghost.

Will Alice's troubled spirit ever find contentment, or is it her destiny to wander through All Saints and Murrells Inlet, along the creek, forever?

Many plantation owners had a home near the ocean or inlet, on an island, or in the mountains, where they might go to escape the humid heat of southern summers and the dreaded "swamp fever."

The Hermitage was built in the 1840s by Dr. Allard Belin Flagg, owner of Wachesaw Plantation. It was to be the home of Dr. Flagg's widowed mother and his young sister, Alice. The two-story white house, with its twelve-foot ceilings, polished pine floors and wide front porch, overlooked the tidal creek in Murrells Inlet. The surrounding grounds were made beautiful with moss-hung trees, wild roses, wisteria vines and wide grassy areas.

Alice and her mother were happy with the beauty and comfort of the new house. They spent many hours arranging their rooms, with the help of maids. From Alice's upstairs room, she could see the high tide come in, its waters washing oyster beds, reeds, and marshes, with the blue of the Atlantic Ocean in the distance. She often stared out her window, dreaming of a young man who lived nearby. She had fallen in love with him, although he was not a member of the rich plantation society to which the Flaggs belonged. But they met from time to time.

Alice's maid sometimes brought her messages from the young man. Then Alice, excited and starry-eyed, would ride her horse across the causeway to the beach to secretly meet her love. It was a happy summer for Alice, and she blossomed into a real beauty. Dr. Flagg mused and wondered about arranging an early marriage for this headstrong young woman whom he loved dearly. He wanted her to have a good life.

When Dr. Flagg learned about the affair, he was bitterly angry with Alice, her maid, the young man, and even his mother. He felt sure his mother could have kept a closer watch on her daughter. He immediately swept Alice off to boarding school in Charleston, putting an end to secret meetings. It was a heartbreaking time for Alice. She took with her a long white dress that she hoped to be married in.

The grave of Alice Flagg
Courtesy of Barry McGee

In Charleston, Alice tried to settle in the school and please her brother. Unfortunately she soon fell ill with the swamp fever. It was the curse of the beautiful coastal lands, which included boggy swamps and stagnant waters. No one knew the cause of the virulent fever, or its cure. The school officials sent for Dr. Flagg as Alice's condition worsened. He came, prepared to take her home to the Hermitage. The long slow journey was hard on anyone, especially a sick person. When they reached Murrells Inlet, the sick, unhappy young woman was unconscious. Her mother had gone to Asheville, North Carolina with friends.

While she was being undressed and put to bed, Alice's engagement ring was found, hanging from a chain around her neck. Dr. Flagg's love and concern for his dear sister instantly turned to bitter rage. Snatching the ring from her neck, he stalked outside and threw it as far as he could into the dark waters of the salt marsh.

When she regained consciousness, Alice knew that her ring was missing. She moaned and cried, begging her faithful maid to please find her ring for her. Beside the bed sat her brother, his anger gone, his head bowed in his hands. He knew the ring could never be found. A swift messenger went to the mountains to bring Alice's mother home. The doctor spent many hours with his sister, attempting to save her life. It was a sad day for the Flagg family and Murrells Inlet when Alice breathed her last breath.

Hers was a legacy of lost love, an unfinished poem or song. It was a love story with a tragic ending.

The house still stands in Murrells Inlet, at a new location. The original site on the creek has been sold and developed, with several lovely new homes.

Mr. and Mrs. Clarke A. Willcox, Sr. of Marion, South Carolina bought the Hermitage and moved there in 1910 with son Clarke, Jr.

and daughter Genevieve. Clarke and "Gen" grew up loving the house and everything about Murrells Inlet. They listened to stories told by old-timers, visited old abandoned houses, and looked for ghostly lights and other world beings. They confidently expected to see Alice in their own home, and included her in conversations when they entered her upstairs room.

Clarke, Jr., "Mr. Clarke," as everyone in Murrells Inlet called him in later years, inherited the house. He collected and retold the sightings of Alice. He could imagine how beautiful she was and how she looked, but he never actually saw her himself.

His aunt came to visit and spent a night in Alice's room. When she looked in the mirror in the shadowy morning light, Alice's ghostly face stared back at her. She vowed never to bother Alice again.

Other family members and friends also claimed to have seen Alice's ghost. Some saw her in the upstairs front bedroom, or on the stairs, or along the creek and marsh, or in the cemetery. Always they described her as an apparition in a long white dress, her dark hair like a cloud on her shoulders, with a sad, worried expression on her face.

With his wife, Miss Lillian, Mr. Clarke often received guests on their spacious porch. The couple repeated these stories and others, and showed the house and Alice's room to anyone interested in their resident ghost.

Mr. Clarke said he always knew that Alice was close to him, and that she loved the Hermitage as he did. He died in 1989 at the age of 93. He is remembered as the "Ghost Story Curator of the Hermitage." He also left many poems and writings, including the book, *Musings of a Hermit.*

The Willcox's four daughters decided, after Mr. Clarke's death, to move the classic old home to another part of the original plantation and sell the valuable waterfront property. The Hermitage is listed in *The National Register of Historic Places.*

The old house, filled with memories, sits dreaming on its new site at the end of Chandler Drive in Murrells Inlet. It is now the property of Joe Chandler, Mr. Clarke's nephew. He and his wife have restored the house and landscaped new grounds for their retirement home. It will no longer be open to the public.

Perhaps Alice moved with the Hermitage to the lovely new site. Or perhaps you will meet her on some dark, lonely night along the waterfront, near the original site of her home.

The Hermitage, home of Alice
Courtesy of J. K. Floyd

2

GHOST DANCERS

ON THE HIGH SAND DUNES

From the ancient past come stories of Native American customs and ceremonies, legends and lore that cannot be well-documented. Yet such tales are interesting to hear or read about.

The wax myrtle bush, for which Myrtle Beach was named, grew profusely along the Grand Strand and into the fringing forest. Indian tribes, living close to nature, developed rites and customs which they clung to year after year, century after century. They looked forward eagerly to the coming of spring, and celebrated a festival of fertility on the sixth day of the new moon in our month of March.

On that date, bonfires built just back of the dunes were piled high with branches of "sacred plants": myrtle, laurel, yaupon and holly. A strong herbal brew was passed from hand to hand, among the older ones. They concocted the brew from the leaves and bark of the sacred plants. Its taste was bitter and harsh, and it was probably extremely strong with caffeine.

As the bonfires blazed ever higher, the adult Indians began to dance, one by one or in couples. The children followed their example. As they danced, the Indians chanted messages to gods of nature, asking for fertility and abundant natural gifts. When the fire burned down to smoldering ashes, the group dispersed. Mothers gathered their children, and men silently watched the remains of the fire. Then the families disappeared into the surrounding forests, with optimism and hope for the new year.

In the fall, they came again to the seashore to perform a similar ceremony. While the fires burned, they danced and chanted with different messages: thanksgiving for the gifts of the year, expulsion of evil, and destruction of their enemies. Early the next morning, the men came to scatter the ashes and debris of the fires on the outgoing tide, to carry away the evils of their world.

Many centuries have passed since these celebrations were practiced. Yet there are some who say the Ghost Dancers of the Sand Dunes can still be seen along the coast.

Certainly you would not look for the dancers on the beach in front of brightly-lit hotels or the pavilion. Look for a deserted strip of lonely beach, through a misty fog at twilight, just between daylight and dark. As you stand far back of the high dunes, watch and wait for a gentle sea breeze to blow tendrils of fog ashore. Wait for a special combination of fog and mist, with salt-laden moisture blown in from the rolling sea. Tall sea wheat plumes along the sand dunes beckon to those long departed spirits.

As the pearl gray twilight deepens, skittering birds hush their chirping, and all is silent except the sounds of the ocean. And then the coils of mist and fog rise and swirl over the dunes and salt marshes.

Suddenly a parade of illusory, shadowy figures move in an ancient ceremonial dance. Perhaps the sea wheat plumes give substance to the figures, but for the moment it is all there, the color and pageantry of ancient native ceremonies, passed down through the centuries. It is a moment to remember.

There are those who would say the Ghost Dancers of the Dunes have returned to this beloved place.

3

THE LEGEND OF THE SEEWEE INDIANS

Flames leaped high as the women threw on broken pieces of wood and bark. Their bonfire blazed atop a tall sand dune close to the broad sandy beach. Beyond stretched the blue waters of the Atlantic Ocean, desolate and empty of any sign of long Indian canoes.

But the fire must be kept burning, night after night, as they had promised the men. Even the small children helped, dragging tree limbs, pine cones and trash to the water's edge to feed the fire.

As the women busied themselves, the unspoken question among them was: "How long will it be before our men return?"

For countless centuries Indian tribes had roamed the Coastal Plain, their simple lifestyle undisturbed. The Seewee tribe's village lay south of Winyah Bay (present-day Georgetown) between the Santee River and the beach. Other tribes lived close by, with similar languages and customs. They found bountiful game in the forests, fish, crabs and oysters in coastal streams, and wild grain, berries and roots for food. It was their special place, where they could pursue life skills handed down from ancient generations.

And then in the late 1600s came the traders and settlers, and life would never be the same again. The settlers cut trees for their cabins and burned and cleared fields. They wanted little contact with the Indians.

The traders brought cheap trinkets, bright beads and calico to tempt the women, and whistles and toys for the children. Once the men had seen the knives and tools the traders offered, how could they do without them? It was extremely hard to resist the new products. The Indians offered rich furs and skins in exchange, worth far more than the items they bought.

Before long, English traders moved freely among the coastal tribes, trading cheap products. The Indians soon realized the difference and asked the traders for fairer prices. They were told they had to trade by the rules. Who made the rules? The Great White Father, the mighty king, who lived across the waters in England. The Indians would have to talk to the king.

The Seewee Tribal Council met and discussed this information. What should they do? Finally they decided to make plans for the voyage across the Great Waters, their name for the ocean. They would build the biggest boats they could and go and see the king. They planned to show him their rich furs and tell him their problems with the traders.

The Indians implicitly believed what the traders had told them as a cruel joke.

Of course, it took the men quite awhile to burn and scrape out several cypress canoes, some of them twenty feet long. Everyone helped. As they worked, the Indians looked constantly toward the far horizon. The trip would be a great adventure. Not many miles away, they expected to find England and visit the Great King. Surely he would understand their problems and help them. What stories they would tell when they returned.

At last the day came when the canoes were completed. Everyone helped load them with their finest furs and skins. The women and children watched proudly as their strongest and most capable men sailed away.

The boats disappeared from sight. The women and children confidently expected the men to return soon. They would wait for them, burning their fires at night to guide the men back home.

As the days and weeks went by, the women were puzzled but they kept on hoping and continued their beach vigil. More moons passed, and still there was no sign of the men. Gradually the waiting group grew smaller, and finally the nightly fires ceased. They all realized they could not survive without the elders and braves of their tribe. Who would make important decisions or defend them when attacked by warriors from other tribes? Leaving was a hard decision to make, but some women and children began to join other nearby tribes. Stormy winter weather was upon them, and they needed food. Others grieved for the men and continued to stay as long as they could, building the bonfire once in awhile.

Unfortunately the men had left on their voyage in early fall, the season of storms and hurricanes. Before many days had passed, they ran into a violent tropical storm. Their cumbersome canoes tossed and turned in the mighty winds. In spite of all they could do, the canoes began to sink. A few survivors were picked up by English ships in the area. When the English sailors pieced together the amazing story the Indians told, they promptly sold them as slaves in the Caribbean.

Sadly, the Seewee elders and braves would never return to their beautiful Coastal Plain homeland. The little village between the Santee River and the beach lay deserted. The women, full of hope and pride when the men left, had taken the children and gone away.

Drifting sand and falling leaves, blown by cold winter winds and rain, soon covered the tiny village nestled among the tall grasses. Finally there appeared no sign that the Seewee village had ever existed. The Seewee Tribe was almost forgotten–but not quite. Their story was told and passed down, to become an Indian legend, still remembered after three hundred years.

Thomas Lynch, Senior built his plantation home on the Santee River in 1740. He named it "Hopsewee," combining the name of the tribe with the name of Chief Hop, a Cherokee Indian. The United Methodist Retreat near Awendaw is called Seewee Coastal Retreat of South Carolina. Seewee State Park, beyond McClellan-ville, hosts hikes and tours to the Waterway and Bull Island. Seewee Restaurant prints a version of the Seewee story on menus.

The tragic story of the Seewee Indians was not forgotten.

Who's to say if ghostly fires still flicker on the beach from time to time, when night winds blow and fog shrouds the high dunes? The faithful women still wait.

*   *   *

Note: A devastating hurricane was recorded as occurring in the year 1699 in *The History of South Carolina*, by Mary C. Simms-Oliphant, to give credence to the legend.

4

SAILING UNDER THE
JOLLY ROGER FLAG
1700s

The young man stood atop a high sand dune looking out to sea. He glimpsed the hazy silhouettes of sailing vessels along the horizon, blurred by distance and the bright sunshine. Along this lonely stretch of Carolina beach, gleaming white sand met the surging blue Atlantic as far as eye could see, a picture-perfect strand.

It had been a restful few days ashore, in spite of the hard work of repairing the ship and looking for fresh water and supplies. Now the men were becoming restless and he knew it was time to go. They thrived on the excitement of the chase, the battle, the victory at sea, and so did he.

The young man and his crew were pirates, prowling along the Carolina coast. Their swift ship sailed under the black flag, flaunting the dreaded skull and crossbones. In the 1700s sailing ships were commonplace offshore, lying low in the distance, or moving into Little River, Southport, or Murrells Inlet with the rising tide. Too often, some of them were pirate ships.

The Jolly Roger flag was first used by French buccaneers. It was rumored that they dyed the flag red with their victims' blood, and called it "Joli Rouge" (pretty red). English pirates mispronounced the name, calling it the Jolly Roger. Blackbeard's flag showed a devil's skeleton on a black flag, with an hourglass in one hand and a spear in the other, pointing to a heart.

A favorite trick of pirates was to fly the flag of England as they approached another ship. When close enough to hail the ship, they lowered the English flag and raised their own Jolly Roger. Helpless merchant ships were caught unawares and quickly captured. Rich cargoes were taken and sometimes hidden or buried.

The fact that pirates attacked ships leaving Charleston and Wilmington is well-documented. Even in the early 1700s, ships loaded with skins and furs sailed from Carolina ports, bound for England. Pirates boldly moved into ports or attacked ships at sea, taking what they wanted and dumping the rest of the cargo. Often they scuttled the ships, leaving crew and passengers to the mercy of the sea. The pirates had the upper hand, demanding shore privileges and supplies from small, weak settlements that had no defense.

Referred to as "the hungriest Caribbean sharks," by William Howard Guess in *S.C. Annals of Pride and Protest*, pirates found the coastline of the Carolinas a fairly safe refuge after battles at sea. Even the most wicked and bloodthirsty of men need fresh water and supplies, as well as a place to repair damaged ships. They knew how to "careen" the ships in narrow, shallow swashes and inlets in order to repair or scrape and caulk the hull of a vessel. Careening, or leaning the wooden ship against a sandy bank, made repairs possible. They floated the ship out again on a high tide.

The British navy patrolled the coast out beyond the continental shelf with some success. Many pirates were captured and hanged for their deeds. Still, the pirates knew all the swashes, inlets, deeper channels, and ports where they could lie low and rest.

Possibly two thousand different pirates preyed on coastal towns and trade for about fifty years. Of these, only a few are well-remembered. Captain Kidd, Blackbeard, Stede Bonnet and others used the islands of Little River and Murrells Inlet when they needed to hide for awhile. Interest in buried treasure perks up when someone prints a pirate map of possible locations, and the stories are told again.

A favorite story in Murrells Inlet, vouched for by old-timers, has become a legend. According to Captain Mack Oliver, long-time keeper of legends and honored teller of tales, Blackbeard was an Inlet visitor in the late 1600s and early 1700s, until his death in 1718. He favored the deserted cove for brief stays and temporary burial of valuable booty. Pirates found no opposition from the few frightened settlers, who lived in mortal fear of such visits.

On one visit, the ship was overloaded with heavy casks of stolen rum, a trophy from the Caribbean Islands. In order to sail swiftly, ships had to lighten their cargo. Blackbeard decided to bury some of the rum on a small island near the mouth of Murrells Inlet, along with a chest of other treasure. So he sailed into the Inlet and set part of his crew to digging, while others gathered oysters and shrimp.

When they finished the work, the pirates proceeded to feast on the succulent roasted oysters and fresh boiled shrimp. The entire crew drank as much rum as they wanted, in a wild night of celebration. Sometime during the night the pirates fell asleep, not knowing or caring where they slept in their drunken state.

One crew member named Jack crawled under some myrtle bushes and scrub palmettos for shelter, back of the dunes. There he made his bed and there he slept, unnoticed by his mates when they awoke the next morning and sailed away. Perhaps they were as befuddled as Jack when they were roused. They left the small lonely island to the sea gulls, the sand creatures, and Jack. They had to sail on the high tide. No one missed Jack until they were far out at sea.

They recalled his eating and drinking with them and singing their ribald songs, but no one saw him boarding the ship. They assumed that Old Jack could look out for himself, so why worry? They would pick him up on their next trip to the inlet island.

Blackbeard's ship sailed on toward the Caribbean, attacking other ships. The crew gave little thought to Jack and Murrells Inlet. So he was abandoned.

Back on the island near Murrells Inlet, Jack finally awoke. The confused pirate raised his aching head and looked around at the bright sunshine. Why was it so quiet? The last thing he remembered was wild laughter and singing and dancing around the bonfire. He and his mates must have guzzled gallons of rum. Even Blackbeard himself had entered into the fun.

But why was he alone, except for the sea gulls? The others must be asleep too. Soon his groggy head sank on this chest and his eyes closed again in drunken sleep.

When Blackbeard and his crew returned two years later, they expected to pick up Jack and retrieve some of the rum. They found the mouth of Murrells Inlet and the small island, but not Jack or the rum. Instead, they counted thirty-two empty casks, scattered here and there on the sand.

Under the myrtle bushes lay the skeleton of a man, a rum bottle clutched in his arms. They assumed it was their mate, Jack. Had he lived and died in a drunken stupor, alone with the sea creatures, the birds and the elements? The buried treasure chest was missing, another mystery.

Jack's memorial is the name of a small, desolate bit of island in a tidal inlet: Drunken Jack's Island. A popular restaurant across the cove on the waterfront keeps the name alive for interested patrons: Drunken Jack's Restaurant and Lounge. They print a brief version of Jack's story on their brochure for all to read.

No one has ever settled on the half-drowned isle–it belongs to Jack. One wonders if he still watches for the return of Blackbeard's ship and his mates to rescue him.

Three centuries have passed since pirates roamed along the coast, coming into the coves and inlets freely. The days of fearful swash-buckling pirates have faded into the past. The terror of the black flag, the Jolly Roger, no longer hovers over small helpless fishing villages along the coast.

But the tales and legends remain, a part of the heritage of bygone days.

5

BLACKBEARD

THE FIERCEST PIRATE OF THEM ALL

Surely his sins were as black as the coarse grizzled beard which gave him his nickname. Few people remember, or ever knew, the pirate's real name (Edward Drummond), but for over three hundred years the name Blackbeard has remained famous. Hugh F. Rankin, renowned historian, considered him "the fiercest pirate of them all." His activities over a scant five years proved his title.

Blackbeard started out as a merchant seaman from Bristol, England. In Queen Anne's War against France, 1702-1713, he served on a privateer which preyed on French shipping in the Caribbean. In the islands he admired the way numerous pirates swaggered around with their ill-gained wealth. In 1713 he joined the crew of a pirate ship and changed his name to Edward Teach. Soon he was captain of his own ship, *Queen Anne's Revenge.* He was set for a life of crime.

The coastline of North and South Carolina offered good hiding places where pirates could careen their ships for necessary repairs. Also Charleston, Georgetown and Wilmington shipped rich cargoes of rice, indigo, furs and skins, and lumber products to England. The Sea Islands, Murrells Inlet, Little River, Southport and the Outer

Banks offered safe havens to restore damages and collect needed ammunition and supplies.

Persistent rumors linked Blackbeard with Colonial Governor Eden of North Carolina; these rumors concerned the offering of payment or "loot" for protection. Blackbeard and twenty of his men asked for the King's pardon, which was available for penitent pirates. For a time Blackbeard lived in a house in Bath, North Carolina, and married a pretty sixteen-year-old girl. She was flattered by attentions from such a famous man. Little did she know that she was wife number fourteen. He treated her shamefully and the marriage was soon over.

A museum in Bath has some items and a chest that may have belonged to Blackbeard during that interlude. He enjoyed the social life and gave extravagant gifts to neighbors. His ships, sheltered in Ocracoke Cove, continued their piracy. He soon grew tired of the tame life in the lovely little town and returned to pirating.

Blackbeard, along with other pirates, was famous for his cruelty to his victims, and to members of his own crew. His acts were so evil that his crew thought he was in league with the devil, or that he was the devil himself. It was a superstitious time. Crew members escaped if they could, but they were afraid the "Devil" would come after them.

Once Blackbeard found a priest among the people on a captured vessel, and brought him on board the pirate ship. He demanded that the trembling young priest conduct Mass for him and his men. One of the men protested and uttered a foul oath. Blackbeard whipped out a pistol and shot the unfortunate seaman dead. As he put his pistol away, he smiled and said, "That'll teach him not to cuss around a priest! Go ahead, Sir!"

The priest, with quavering voice, went on with the service. He must have wondered what fate awaited him.

Another time Blackbeard was drinking in his cabin with Israel Hands and another seaman, both friends of his. Suddenly he picked up two pistols, held them under the table, and began shooting. The other seaman slipped out, but Israel took a full charge in one knee. It left him lame for life. On a trip to England, he was literally dumped ashore, and ended up a beggar on the streets of London.

When asked why he would shoot a friend, Blackbeard explained that he had to shoot one or two of them once in awhile to remind them of who he was.

The Carolinas and Virginia were virtually besieged by Blackbeard and other pirates, and trade came to a standstill. Something had to be done. Blackbeard had humiliated Charleston by capturing nine merchant ships, laden with rich cargoes. He demanded a ransom for the lives of the passengers–a chest filled with medicines, worth about four hundred pounds. He received the chest and freed the crew and passengers, although he took everything they had, including their clothes.

The final attack on Blackbeard came at Ocracoke Cove when two sloops, sent by Governor Spotswood of Virginia, approached the pirate's hideout. Captain Ellis Brand was in charge of the mission, and Lieutenant Robert Maynard commanded the larger sloop.

Blackbeard was a fearsome sight when ready for battle. A tall, powerful man, he armed himself with loaded pistols, primed for instant firing, daggers, cutlass and sword. He plaited his long bushy beard in pigtails, and tucked among them the long, slow-burning matches used to light the cannon. When he attacked, he lit the matches. Smoke swirled around him, striking terror in his victims, who also thought he must be the devil himself.

In the final battle, Lt. Maynard confronted the pirate, who was surrounded by Maynard's men. Blackbeard was shot twenty-five times, he was stabbed again and again, and his throat was slashed before he fell dead. Maynard's men displayed the pirate's severed head as a trophy on the bowsprit of the sloop.

With the end of Blackbeard, and other pirates, colonial trade gradually resumed. His startling career had only lasted from 1713 until November of 1718, so he was still a young man when he died. Blackbeard held the dubious honor of being the best known of all the pirates hovering along the coast of the colonies.

On dark, misty nights, when great banks of fog roll in from the sea, it is easy to imagine the outline of a sailing vessel along the horizon. It is often said that spirits of the pirates look for their buried treasures near the swashes and inlets. Perhaps Blackbeard searches for his massive head. That's a terrifying thought: a headless pirate, seeking his lost head as well as his ship and rich treasure!

The cries of those who lost their lives from the cruel treatment of heartless pirates rise up on the winds that blow, a keening sound. The sorrow and seeking never cease, even three centuries later. It is unfinished business, unpunished crime, and the memories do not let go easily.

It was a ghostly era, when bloodthirsty pirates roamed the seas and the coast. Each year at Halloween, the stories come to life again at Atalaya, "Castle in the Sand," the winter home of the Huntingtons, founders of Brookgreen Gardens. Eerie sounds and ghostly lights are part of the show. Blackbeard himself usually puts in an appearance, to the delight of those watching. It is a real Halloween experience to hear the cries and see the actors in the darkness of the empty rooms playing the parts of long-departed pirates. It is the time of year for ghostly experiences.

6

THE HANGING TREE

It is a name to strike terror in the heart, even after more than two and a half centuries–"The Hanging Tree!" The name brings to mind images of brutal death, of frontier justice, of avid watchers. What if the wrong person was executed? It happened.

The name is used, still today, for a tall, stately cypress tree standing beside U. S. Highway 17-A. The road branches away from the King's Highway, the coastal road, southwest of Georgetown. Local people call Highway 17-A "Saints' Delight Road," for the church close by.

The cypress must have been a sturdy tree even in the 1770s, when the first known hanging took place. All around, ancient oaks and other native trees along the roadside still survive. The road to Jamestown has been in use since early days of settlement.

Frontier justice, without benefit of judge or jury, was considered swift and sure, although the justice part was always debatable.

A public hanging was not a pretty sight. Yet accounts tell of large crowds gathering, including women and children. They watched wide-eyed, children clutching their mothers' skirts in shock and fear. Perhaps it would be a deterrent to would-be criminals.

In the late 1770s, the Revolution divided families and friends, Tories against Patriots, as the war continued. British ships occupied the port of Georgetown; soldiers patrolled the town and countryside. Without the use of the port, the Patriots found commodities scarce and food in great demand. Two Patriot soldiers, trying to find food, were surprised by a Tory (a British sympathizer and former neighbor) who shot them dead. To his surprise, he was quickly surrounded by a band of Patriots.

They had seen exactly what happened. They asked no questions and lost no time capturing the Tory. Someone quickly found a rope and the hanging took place immediately, from the limb of the cypress tree.

Through the years, many other hangings took place. In the late 1800s, after the Civil War, hangings still occurred. They were, in effect, lynchings. Even so, it seems there was an unofficial "lynch law," which covered such punishments. No one asked many questions, and the practice continued, as terrible as it seems.

The road ran along the outskirts of the little community of Lamberttown, where families had strong ties. They looked out for each other and asked for little help from the outside. As for their children and young people, very little "foolin' around" took place. If young couples were "courting," it probably led to marriage. There was no alternative. Everyone understood that.

And then came a stranger, strong, good looking, with an eye for the girls. He had evidently never heard of the strict rules the young people of Lamberttown lived by. He had eyes for all the girls, but he finally settled on a lovely one, sweet and pretty and naive.

Surely wedding bells would ring soon in Saints' Delight Church. It was confidently expected by the community.

To the amazement of everyone, it was not long before the cry went out that the worst crime had been committed. Worst of all, the young man was leaving, not marrying.

The men of the community lost no time catching the young man and bringing him back. No need to notify the law in Georgetown—they knew just what to do. The angry men brought the young fellow to the Hanging Tree, where a crowd was already gathering. Someone had the long rope ready and placed the noose over his head, throwing the end of the rope over a limb of the old cypress tree. Another man drove a horse and wagon in place and forced the young man to climb up and stand in the wagon bed.

Several men pulled on the long rope as the horse dashed away with the wagon. The young man was lifted clear of any support. Almost at the same moment a massive thunderstorm arose, with frightening thunder, lightning, rain and strong winds. As people scattered, the young man desperately freed his head from the noose and fell to the ground.

Off he ran into the surrounding woods and thickets, never to be seen again. The men searched the area and found no trace of him. He had been properly hanged by experts. No one had ever survived before. What could have happened? Who was the young man? Was he the devil himself? Maybe that was why they couldn't kill him. And the stories grew over the years. When strangers heard the tale they were afraid to go under the "hanging limb." Maybe there was something magical or evil about the tree itself.

Years later, the road was paved and traffic increased. Hangings had long since ceased, but the tree still stood, with its threatening limb hanging over the road. Those who remembered the stories wondered how many had died by hanging. No one had kept such a fearful count. It was not something you talked about with pride.

One night a high-bodied truck went speeding down the dark, lonely stretch of road and hit the overhanging limb. With a sound like thunder, the limb cracked away from the great tree. The men of Lamberttown immediately gathered around and had the driver arrested for defacing their famous landmark.

Feelings ran high when the driver was let out of jail without even paying a fine. Everyone thought he should have "done time." Needless to say, he left quickly, never to return, like a certain other young man. People greatly resented the damage done to their famous or infamous tree, the scene of so many lynchings.

Even without the "hanging limb," the tree is easy to recognize. It stands close by Highway 17-A, beyond the Lamberttown sign. To some travelers who know the story, the place has an aura of mystery and death, of heightened energy from lives cut short. It is a place to be avoided.

People often went to Georgetown to sell produce or buy necessities. Coming back in late afternoon by slow horse and wagon, some were reluctant to pass under the old tree, especially in the gloom of early dusk. Some preferred to go around by Andrews instead of passing near the tree.

Why? Have you seen anything? No, it was just a feeling, a creepy spine-tingling feeling, of looking out for what you might see. You had to keep your eyes open, just in case. Moss moving in the breeze and fog drifting inland from Winyah Bay did not help your feelings.

If you are not afraid to pass under the tree, watch for the Lamberttown sign—you will recognize the Hanging Tree.

7

A LIGHT IN THE WINDOW

Just south of the Horry County beaches lies the oldest fishing village in South Carolina, according to honored story tellers: Murrells Inlet. Some resident families are descendants of early plantation owners and still follow a lifestyle dictated by birth and heritage. Other hardy souls follow the traditions of seafaring men, totally dependent on the ocean tides. Their boats can cross the bar, from inlet to ocean, at high tide only, with the depth of water a scant nine feet. They come and go with nature's permission.

Yet the fishing fleets supply a bounty of food for the many restaurants of this gracious "Seafood Capital" of the state. Novice fishermen try their hands with the deep sea fishing fleet, hoping to avoid sunburn and seasickness, and bring home a catch.

Along the marshy creek, giant moss draped oak trees spread their branches over homes and grounds. Tall old houses line the embankment, facing toward the Atlantic Ocean. Planters built a few homes before the Revolutionary War, in the 1770s, and others before the Civil War. Plantation families hastened to the beaches or retreated to the mountains in the humid hot summers. Murrells Inlet and Garden City Beach (today) offered popular escapes, along with Pawleys Island.

Many of the old homes still stand, in varying states of disrepair. Others have been lovingly kept and stand somewhat aloof from the newer "condos," houses that have sprung up in the last twenty years. Names like Vauxhall, Wachesaw, the Hermitage, Woodland, Sunnyside and Belin Memorial Methodist Church bring to mind many families and events of the past. Dignified and beautiful, these early homes were so sturdy and well-built they have survived both the storms and the wars of two centuries.

The Heriot family, of Mount Arena Plantation, built Woodlands as a summer residence before the Revolutionary War. It served as a comfortable home and a wonderful playground for generations of families through the years. The clapboard siding, the wide veranda and white columns marked Woodlands as a typical Inlet home. Wide windows and ocean breezes cooled the house in its location along Woodlands Creek. Moss-draped oaks surrounded the lawns and flower beds.

The third floor had a central window over the entrance which gave a lofty view of the Inlet and the blue Atlantic Ocean beyond. Over the years, Woodlands changed owners several times. In the 1840s, it became the home of a Murrells Inlet sea captain and his family. He placed a small telescope in the third floor window and taught his children to use it carefully. Needless to say, the room became a magical play space for them.

The captain did not own a ship but piloted the ships of others on fishing trips or longer voyages to faraway places. He became known as a man of sound judgment and experience. When he went away on a trip, his loving family watched and waited and counted the days until his return.

When a wealthy planter bought a three-masted schooner from Scotland, the captain was given the job of bringing it home. The ship was beautifully crafted and outfitted, and the captain longed to own it.

After several years the owner died and the captain was able to buy the ship from the estate. Proudly he brought the splendid schooner home to Murrells Inlet and Woodlands Creek. His wife and children shared his pride and excitement.

Now he could charter longer fishing trips, or sail to the Caribbean Islands or to New York or New England. It was a new phase of his work.

Hurricanes were especially hazardous for sailing vessels, and they often blew up without warning. Late in September, a powerful storm caught the boat moored in the narrow creek. Realizing the ship would be battered and buffeted by the winds, the captain decided to sail out into the open sea at the mouth of the inlet. The family dreaded to see him go. His wife promised to keep a lamp burning in the high third floor window to guide him home. And she did, watching for the ship's running lights as the captain anchored the boat in the raging Atlantic. All night she watched, only to see the lights disappear.

Perhaps he had moved farther out to sea to be safer. His wife would not be discouraged, but kept her light burning, night after night. She scarcely slept. The calm waters of the sea and inlet brought hope each day that he would sail in. And so, the sad, worried family waited for the captain.

On the anniversary of the ship's disappearance, she thought she saw the running lights again and waited happily for the ship. It never came in. Although the family was deeply discouraged, they never gave up. She taught her children that they must never lose hope.

The children accepted her words and helped in every way they could. Gradually they became aware that neighbors and friends looked askance at the lamp burning in the upper window, shaking their heads and murmuring to each other. Other children grinned at them and asked, "Has your Pa come home yet?"

Yet the wife remained true to her promise, which had become a vow: she would keep her light burning each night in the upper room to guide her dear husband home.

The children grew up and went away. The frail, elderly wife remained at Woodlands alone, climbing the stairs each night. She lit the lamp and searched the mouth of the Inlet with dimming eyes–to no avail. She would not leave Woodlands.

After her death, the house was abandoned and empty, as so many homes were after the Civil War. Curiously enough, fishermen through the years reported seeing a glimmering light in the attic window. When the fishermen investigated, they found no one, and no lamp or candle. But as they looked back, the lamp was glowing brighter than ever in the attic window. Beyond the mouth of the Inlet they caught a glimpse of the running lights of a ship.

It was the anniversary of the September storm, so long ago.

After Woodlands burned down, the story was almost forgotten in the village of Murrells Inlet. But such stories have a way of surviving and become a tale to tell on a dark stormy night, when few ships would dare to cross the bar.

As the story is told to a group of listeners, you might look for a ghostly ship's light, hovering at the mouth of the Inlet. On the anniversary of that long ago hurricane, you might also see the light of a lamp flickering among the trees where Woodlands once stood.

As the captain looks for a light in the window, his faithful wife is still trying to guide him home.

8

THE ROCKING CHAIR

John Henry reined in his horse as he moved along Georgetown's Front Street toward the apothecary shop. The stores backed up to the Sampit River, which flowed into Winyah Bay and on out to sea. It was a short scenic river, with town houses beyond the shops and plantation homes farther out. The river was filled with local traffic. The streets of the town were lined with spreading oak trees that offered shelter from the sun's hot rays. Small groups of people stood talking and visiting under their welcome shade, but John Henry scarcely noticed anyone who looked at him or called out a greeting. Instead of a pleasant expression, his handsome face wore an anxious look as he considered his personal problem.

The year was 1830. John Henry had ridden his horse hard along the King's Highway from Hampton Plantation, a distance of about sixteen miles. He was on a desperate decision-making journey that meant everything to him. He had slipped away from home early to come into town alone.

John Henry Rutledge, twenty-one years old and heir to Hampton Plantation, was in love. The pretty young daughter of the town pharmacist had caught his eye. Consequently, he took advantage of every opportunity to ride into Georgetown to see and talk to her. Not only was she a "winsome lass," but she was educated and well-mannered. He considered her far superior to the plantation belles he had known all his life.

Except John Henry knew the rules of society by which he lived. One of the most important rules was that none of the young people married beneath them. It was a carry-over from the rigid class system in England, and no one in plantation society questioned the system. A wife should be able to take her proper place, to entertain and be entertained, with grace and dignity. John Henry had accepted the rules—until he fell in love with a shop-keeper's daughter. Surely there were exceptions, he told himself as he approached the shop.

He had talked to his mother, long and earnestly, about his love for the girl. Surely she would understand. Instead his mother, Harriott Horry Rutledge, was horrified at the thought of such a marriage. She reminded him that his duty to the family name was to make a "good" marriage. He was the eldest son and heir to the great Hampton estate.

Harriott herself had married late, when she was almost thirty. Her mother, Harriott Pinckney Horry, had greatly feared that her only daughter would be a spinster. Instead, the girl unexpectedly eloped with Frederick Rutledge. Soon she was busy grooming a large family of children, four boys and four girls. In the home, her word was law, and the children acted accordingly.

Everyone seemed to be against John Henry. He clinched his fists as he took care of his horse and approached the small apothecary shop on Front Street in Georgetown. He planned to have a serious talk with the pharmacist about loving his daughter. He wanted to marry his dear little "Lady Love" anyway and take her home to Hampton. When his family got to know her, they would learn to love her too. He was certain his plan would work.

With this in mind, John Henry squared his shoulders and entered the shop. He was a man with a mission and filled with determination and courage. In his immaturity, he could see only his point of view, so he expected cooperation and understanding from the father and the girl's family.

When the pharmacist was free, John Henry poured out the whole story, how he felt, what his mother had said, and the way his siblings had teased him.

As he talked, the pharmacist became very angry. He was a well-educated man, proud of his shop and his family. People in the town respected him, but he realized his place.

When John Henry finally stopped talking, the pharmacist rejected him, his family, his great estate, and his high and mighty plan. He would never allow his precious daughter to marry into a family that would look down on her or, at best, tolerate her.

"And, sir," he continued, "you are no longer welcome in my shop or on my side of Front Street. I am warning you not to speak to my daughter again. For your information, she has other plans!

"Good day to you, sir."

John Henry was politely ushered out of the little shop. The tables were turned. John Henry could scarcely believe it. Sadly, he rode back to Hampton in a state of shock. Imagine, a Rutledge spurned!

When he reached home, John Henry wearily climbed the stairs and entered his room, located to the right of the landing. He pulled his rocking chair over to the window so he could gaze at the beautiful fields of home that he had always loved. He had grown up knowing he would someday be master here.

Except now there was no joy for the young man. He dropped his head into his hands. Tears wet his cheeks. Life seemed empty indeed. He sat there, nursing his grief, as well as his anger at the entire world. He had discovered that life was not fair.

The brothers and sisters were no help at all. They teased and taunted John Henry with their remarks:

"Why don't you grow up and stop acting like a child?"

"You're young! You should have lots of girls before you marry."

"Find another girl—there's lots of them around!"

"Who do you think you are, to try to change the rules?"

Any family has a bit of sibling jealousy, and the Rutledges had theirs, especially toward the heir-apparent of the rich Hampton estate. John Henry sat stony-faced, while his brothers and sisters enjoyed their teasing.

After several days, the family tired of his depression. They decided to ignore him as he sat in his rocker. His mother and father refused to look at him, although they worried about his state of mind and health.

It was the night of March 30, 1830. The family and friends had gathered in the candle-lit ballroom for music and dancing. They had urged John Henry to join them, but he simply turned aside. So they left him alone with his broken heart. No one understood. No one cared. He sat by his window, listening to the music and light chatter.

After the party ended, the rain began. John watched in the semi-darkness as the wind and rain swept in from the Santee River Delta. All nature seemed to be weeping with him. That was when he came to a tragic decision.

He had secretly kept a small pistol under the cushions of his rocking chair. No one knew he had it. As he fumbled for the gun, the quiet house waited, with the fair fields of his plantation home awash in the storm. Suddenly a shot rang out. John Henry's body sagged to the floor. His blood spilled on the floor boards from the bullet wound in his head.

The family sent for the doctor, who told them that the bullet was deep in John Henry's brain, and nothing could be done. They gathered round their dying son and brother, offering tearful assurances that they loved him. John Henry rallied briefly, and even smiled at his loved ones, seeming to beg for their forgiveness.

Two days later he died. He was laid to rest in a corner of the garden, facing the river. They marked his grave with a white marble slab.

But John Henry's troubled spirit has not rested. Many people have felt his presence in the room where he sat. From time to time his chair rocks, with no one there. The bloodstains have been cleaned from the floorboards many times, but each time they reappear.

His is still a restless ghost. Perhaps he returns seeking the love and understanding he missed as a callow youth, bent on having his way at all costs. His siblings might advise him:

"Give it up, John Henry! Rest in peace."

* * *

This was the story told to us by Professor Archibald Rutledge, our host. He was the owner of the great estate of Hampton Plantation and a direct descendant of the Rutledge family from the early 1700s. It was an honor to have him conduct our tour of his home.

My eighth-grade students and I were enjoying a planned field trip to the great plantation on the banks of the Santee River.

My students stood on the stairs and landing outside John Henry's room, with his rocking chair in full view. No one volunteered to go inside or sit in the chair. All faces were serious, all eyes focused on

Professor Rutledge as he recounted the story of the young man's death. Young and rich, heir to the estate, John Henry decided he could not live without the young woman he loved so he took his own life. It was a tragic story.

Rutledge told us that the chair rocks from time to time, with no one there. Attendants have found the chair pulled over to the window, where John Henry liked to sit and look out over the fields and rice channels of Hampton. Attendants downstairs often feel a presence or hear the chair rocking. People visiting the house on tours sometimes have one who is sensitive to "beings," usually a lady, and she will ask a question or make a remark that shows her awareness.

Professor Rutledge returned to Hampton in 1937 when he retired from teaching in Pennsylvania. His purpose was to restore the beautiful house and grounds, which had stood vacant for many years. It was the ancient home of his ancestors, having been in his family since 1686.

Rutledge died in 1973, when he was almost ninety years old. He knew that his work at Hampton had been worthwhile. To insure that the house and plantation would be cared for, he conveyed it to the state of South Carolina. After he died at his home in the town of McClellanville, his funeral was held on the front portico of Hampton. It was attended by friends, colleagues, and dignitaries from across the nation.

The Native Son had returned. He had come home to Hampton, his beloved "Home by the River."

Rutledge, gifted writer, Poet Laureate of South Carolina for many years, was buried in the little cemetery near the river, in the corner of the garden. Several family members, including John Henry, are buried there also.

9

ESTHER AND PIERRE

She sat on a bench near the portico of St. James Santee Parish Church, absently fingering a fold of her long full skirt. A soft breeze blew tendrils of her greying blonde hair and she smoothed it hurriedly. Her gaze focused toward the south along the strip of highway leading toward McClellanville and Charleston. She seemed to be listening intently for a sound that no one else could hear.

"Come on, Miss Essie! We got to go!" It was the driver of her buggy urging her to return home. He knew she would sit for hours, lost in her thoughts and memories. Always it was the same.

Slowly she rose to her feet and made her way to the buggy. After one last look down the road, she sat with bowed head. She would be back.

*　　*　　*

South Carolina Historical Marker No. 1026 stands near the road in front of St. James Santee Parish Church. It is located on a long stretch of the old King's Highway which, at this point, is not a part of Highway 17. Known earlier as Wambaw Church, this classic building was erected in the 1760s at the request of French Huguenot (Protestant) settlers. In this strange new land, they had found a place to build homes and new lives along the vast Santee River and its delta. Here they were safe from persecution.

The fine old church is located off the Hampton Plantation Road, near the Santee River, between Georgetown and McClellanville. The Church of England established the parish in 1706, the second oldest in the Carolina colony.

The round brick columns on the front portico display the beauty and dignity of this house of worship. Inside, high-backed cypress pews and the mahogany pulpit and altar rail show the rich color and sheen of the durable wood. Every detail of decoration was executed faithfully by gifted artisans. The planters and their families took their religion very seriously and spared no expense in the building.

At first the congregation was a mixed group of French Huguenots and Anglican worshipers, reflecting the background of the settlers. Briefly they held separate services, but later merged as Anglicans or Episcopalians.

Traces of history are noted throughout the church. Thomas Lynch's name is carved on a pew, and signatures of other notables from the Revolutionary period can be seen, preserved in glass-fronted cases. The Rev. Samuel Fenner Warren served as parish rector from 1758 until his death in 1789. Miraculously the church escaped desecration and destruction in the Revolution in the 1770s and the Civil War in the 1860s.

Before 1860, the church was also a social center for the large community of plantation owners. On Sunday the churchyard would fill with coaches and carriages, with ladies and gentlemen chatting on the fine portico and entering the sanctuary. They wore the finest clothes and styles of the period, many of them imported from Europe.

Usually people brought hampers of food and enjoyed a bountiful dinner and social hour after the worship service. It was a lively, colorful scene, under the spreading oak trees. It was the place to see friends and hear news of others.

Inevitably young people paired off and strolled together, under the trees and in the cemetery. Never before had tombstones received such close inspection.

Essie, almost sixteen, grew prettier each day. At least tall, handsome Peter thought so, as he watched her unobtrusively. One day he walked beside her and spoke to her. When she lifted shy eyes and smiled at him, he bowed slightly and said, "I'm Pierre."

She whispered back, "I'm Esther." To the rest of their world they were Peter and Essie, but privately they knew each other as Esther and Pierre. They only met on Sundays, but their feelings for each other grew. Essie's dreams were all of Peter.

The young men of the church always rode their spirited thorough-bred horses. The straight road in front of the church offered a great temptation to race, and this was the way the day sometimes ended.

Racing was a favorite sport. Most plantations had a section of road about two miles long, especially prepared for racing. The stretch of Old King's Highway near the church lay straight and smooth and led on to the woods beyond. It was a perfect place for racing to the restless young "blades and scions" of the community. It also seemed to be a safe place. People smiled and shrugged at the enthusiasm of all the young people.

But one Sunday was different. The race began as usual, in front of the church, with everyone waving and calling good wishes. Essie had eyes for no one but Peter. And off they went, down to the far turn. The watchers saw a horse suddenly falter, then fall, throwing the rider against a tree.

The group watched silently, with anxious hearts. Presently a rider pulled away from the other young men and came to the church.

"It's Peter—we think his neck is broken!"

Shock, disbelief, sorrow swept through the crowd. Essie grieved for the days that followed and the sad service for handsome Peter.

Essie never forgot the walks and whispered conversations with Pierre. She dreamed of the life they might have had together. It became more real to her than everyday life. She took care of his grave, but she also watched the far curve at the edge of the woods. Surely if she kept faith he would come galloping up to her one day.

So she listened and waited for the sound of his horse.

* * *

Services in St. James Santee Parish Church ended after the Civil War, which marked the end of the Plantation Era. Today, the centuries-old church is securely fenced and guarded against vandalism. It is opened once a year for worship and homecoming for family descendants. It is a sacred place of gathering, of memories and legends. That day is for remembering old customs and lifestyles.

Some say that the spirits of long ago linger in the churchyard and adjoining cemetery.

If you visit the church, sit in the sunshine awhile. Listen with your heart for the light chatter of beautifully dressed ladies and children and gallant gentlemen, bowing to newcomers. Your imagination leads the way.

Give a thought to shy Essie and Peter, getting acquainted and falling in love as they stroll together. Listen as the organ sounds for dismissal. Young men gather on the road with their horses, joking about the race to come.

Then tragedy strikes, ending life and romance for two young people.

Once again you are alone before the historic old church. The sun glimmers among the trees and old tombstones. A breeze gently lifts the hanging moss in giant oak trees.

And Esther waits for Pierre.

10

TROUBLE AT PEACHTREE PLANTATION

They called it "Carolina Gold," the fine rice that grew in fields along the banks of coastal rivers in South Carolina. It was in great demand in European countries. Before the Civil War, the George-town area plantations produced more rice than any other location in the world. "Rice was king," and the Rice Barons, the planters, were the richest men in America.

The planters built beautiful manor houses and furnished them with imported furniture and ornaments. Their lifestyle rivaled that of the English nobility. They gave little thought to the labor of thousands of slaves who made the rich way of life possible. Many of the sons of the planters went to England for several years of educa-tion, concluding their schooling with travel in Europe, the "Grand Tour." They came home to the leisurely life of a gentleman planter or lawyer, with their fortune assured by the rice crop. Many things changed after the Civil War. Plantations were abandoned by their owners, leaving the fine old houses empty and decaying. The slaves scattered also, not knowing where to go or what to do. Some of them stayed on in their little slave huts, scratching out a few food crops, and fishing or hunting.

If you explore the woods across the South Santee River, you may come across the ruins of a fine old manor house, built in 1762. It is the burned hulk of Peachtree Manor House. Thomas Lynch, Sr., owner of Hopsewee and father of a signer of the Declaration of Independence, decided to move his family across the river to what he considered a more favorable location.

Peachtree Manor House burned in 1840, yet its ruins still stand. You can see the remarkable and careful construction of earlier times, even with the passage of so many years. High brick walls stand with gaping windows. Massive steps and ironwork show expert workmanship. Some remnants of yellow pine timbers escaped the fire. In its time, Peachtree was a palatial home and a fine plantation.

Several years before it burned, another owner and his wife lived there with their lovely eighteen-year-old daughter. She was the joy of their lives, a talented girl with a happy, loving outlook. The slaves loved her; they were always anxious to do her bidding. She grew up playing with them and helping with the household chores.

One day a Spanish ship came sailing up the South Santee River on the high tide, and stopped at Peachtree Landing. It was always exciting to have a ship stop by, especially one from a foreign country.

But this ship was in trouble. One of its young ship's officers was very sick. He desperately needed treatment. The captain asked permission to leave the sick man at Peachtree while the ship went on to Charleston. He promised to return for the seaman in three days.

"But what's wrong with the man?" the planter demanded. "I have no doctor here."

"He's very sick," the captain replied. "He has a bad stomach and high fever. He needs help for a few days." The sick man was closely wrapped in a sheet, and the captain did not mention the red spots already appearing on his body. It was a sign of the dreaded and contagious scarlet fever.

The planter protested, knowing the risks of any illness on the isolated plantation. Just then his daughter came running down to the landing, followed by some of the house servants.

"What is it, Father? Oh! the poor man is so sick! We must try to help him. We have room for him."

The planter reluctantly agreed, but he refused to let the seaman into the main house. He instructed the servants to take the man to the Sick House in the slave village. The seaman began to shake with a chill, and lapsed into a coma. As soon as they saw the red blotches on his skin, they knew they were dealing with scarlet fever.

The planter forbade his daughter from going to the Sick House or helping with the sick man, but she helped anyway. In spite of all they could do, the man died before the three days were up. The ship never came back, so they buried the seaman in the edge of the slave cemetery. The daughter laid a bunch of flowers on the grave and softly whispered a prayer while the slaves finished the burial.

Predictably, about two weeks later the daughter became sick with fever. The distraught father had a doctor come from Charleston and one from Georgetown. They tried to cool her fever, but they had no magic cure for the dread disease. The beloved daughter died. Her parents were inconsolable.

Soon it was evident that the father had lost his mind. He paced back and forth on the great veranda facing the river, raging and ranting at the Spanish ship, at the dead seaman, and even at God, for letting his precious daughter die. Then he barricaded the house and ordered the servants to bar the gates. Grieving neighbors came to offer their sympathy and help, but they were turned away. For days the father held his daughter's body, and watched over her.

Finally the mother persuaded him to fashion a coffin and bury their daughter. The two of them prepared the girl for burial. The father called for several of his slaves, and together they made their way deep into the woods to a small hill above the river the girl had loved all her life. The slaves sat and waited for the father's directions.

He could not bear to put her underground.

Finally he decided to stand the coffin upright and pile dirt around it to make it stable. He and the slaves used their hands to dig as much dirt as they could. For days they worked, piling the dirt higher and higher. They covered the mound to a height of fifteen feet. It was an earthen pyramid in the wilds of the Carolina coast.

Extensive planting encircled the mound, native holly and bay-berry plants, with an outer ring of camellias. Trailing cape jessamine, one of the girl's favorites, grew on the mound itself. As the shrubs grew tall and thick they made an impenetrable barrier to the mound, which was what the father wanted.

And so this burial mound has stood for over a century and a half. It can still be found. The sacred spot remains, a symbol of a father's grief and devotion.

As long as he lived, the father went to the grave and sat for hours, thinking of his daughter's beauty and charm, and mourning her loss. The slaves kept the grave site neat.

After the father died, no one came to the grave. Even hunters avoided it. It was as if the planter's spirit were still there. Anyone exploring the woods spoke of feeling a presence near the site, and a kind of dread. There are those who say that the father still guards the resting place of his precious daughter. He makes it known to visitors that he is there.

It is a troubled story of grief, despair and death at Peachtree Manor. Remember these words, if you visit the site: tormented spirits seldom rest. You may, like others, feel a ghostly presence near the mound.

11

THE SOLDIER ON THE STAIRS

The Henning House, built in 1760, is located at 321 Screven Street, on the corner of Duke Street, in Georgetown. The house, like many others built in the colonial period, copies the Barbadian style. The long side of the house faces the garden, and the narrow side faces the street. The wall of the house extends across the end of the wide, spacious porch and joins the garden wall. A door at the end of the porch allows visitors to enter from the sidewalk. Much of the entertaining in earlier times took place on the piazza, or porch. The plan insured privacy.

During the American Revolution, the English occupied Georgetown since its port was considered useful. Many of the fine old homes of wealthy planters were taken over as quarters for British officers. As a result, the customary social life in Georgetown was at a standstill. Some families had to move out of their town houses or go to their plantations to accommodate the British. This increased their feelings of animosity toward the enemy.

However, a few families were staunch Tories, still loyal to the King. The Tories welcomed the soldiers into their homes. They were given comfortable quarters and the best food and drink, and enjoyed their stay. The Patriots were not so hospitable, doing as little as possible for the British.

The Henning family were Patriots from the time they set foot in this wonderful new land. They had come from an impoverished area in the Homeland and had never before been able to own land. In the Plantation South, a new way of life had developed. Many people received grants of land to cultivate, and they hoped to make a fortune. It was a grand opportunity for most of the European settlers.

The Henning family owned a plantation, and a town house in Georgetown where they spent the hot, humid summers. Two sons fought for the Patriot cause. One daughter, Rosalie, was at home with her father. There were several bedrooms upstairs which the British soldiers could use, and they promptly moved in.

At first, Mr. Henning found it difficult to be nice to his house guests. He was torn between two schools of thought. As a gentleman, he had to act as a generous and welcoming host to the strangers in his home. As a Patriot, he could scarcely stomach the thought. Yet, how could these young lads have caused the war? He pondered the problem for a long time.

Rosalie, Mr. Henning's young and beautiful daughter, soon came to terms with the same problem. The young officers were near her age, friendly, eager to have fun, and unfailingly courteous and helpful to her. They always asked permission to sit on the porch in the heat of the afternoon, and helped with any chore they could. One of them, Guy, soon became a favorite. Often they talked together, sharing experiences and dreams. She worried about Guy when he was out on patrol. How could such a nice friend be an enemy? Was she unfaithful to the Patriot cause?

As they became more intimate, Guy called the girl "Rose." She seemed like a rose to him. With every meeting, they secretly shared their thoughts, and their feelings for each other grew. Mr. Henning must not know, but the other officers could tell how the two felt and helped them keep the secret.

The war intensified in South Carolina in 1780, especially around the port cities. Georgetown and Charleston, and Wilmington in North Carolina, were convenient ports for the British to deliver supplies to the South, where the war effort was concentrated. The elusive Francis Marion and other partisan leaders gathered soldiers wherever they could, to help the Continental Army. These fighters often frustrated the planned attacks of the British. The partisans had no formal training as soldiers, but they were skilled riders and woodsmen. They could slink away into the forests, leaving no trace. The British were accustomed to formal battles, with lines drawn on an open field.

It was a very confused period for everyone. The Georgetown soldiers were called out more and more to search for Patriot partisans. Rosalie worried whenever Guy was away, knowing the risks from the phantom fighters. Surely this war must end soon. She and Guy had spoken of marriage, and a life together. It was what she dreamed of constantly.

Guy and the other officers came to the Henning House early one morning, after a night of patrol, and went upstairs for naps. Rosalie was happy as she helped the cook prepare meals for them when they awakened. Suddenly shots erupted on Duke Street. Horses galloped swiftly on Screven Street, just around the corner. The other officers were up before Guy could shake off his fatigue. He heard someone say that Francis Marion was close by, so he rushed to join the others.

And then it happened. In his haste, Guy forgot the uneven riser near the top of the stairs. He tripped. Rosalie came into the hall just as he fell, tumbling over and over, trying desperately to stop. His head hit hard, breaking his neck. The officers gathered around him, and let Rosalie through. They protected her from the view of others.

What a heartbreak for Guy's friends, and especially for Rosalie. She turned to her father for comfort, and he understood her grief. She told him that Guy had planned to remain in Georgetown when the war was over. Together they arranged for him to be buried privately in the churchyard with a Christian service.

When the British withdrew from Georgetown, it seemed that Guy's spirit stayed behind. He became the keeper of the stairs, a helpful ghost that keeps others from falling as he did. Rosalie often felt his caring spirit, as did many others.

Today the old house sits dreaming on the same corner. The early residents are long gone, as are more recent dwellers. It is a pleasant house, full of memories, lovingly kept for future generations.

Many people have been aware of the ghostly keeper of the stairs, the young British soldier who tragically fell to his death.

12

THEODOSIA

LOVELY MISTRESS OF THE OAKS

"Where is Theodosia?"

It was the poignant, bewildering question asked again and again in 1813. And now, nearly two hundred years later, the question is still unanswered: "What happened to Theodosia?"

Joseph Alston, governor of South Carolina, haunted the docks where his wife had boarded the small ship, *The Patriot*, bound for New York. He asked the same questions of the men there. In Columbia, he sat alone in his quarters, scarcely mindful of his duties.

At their plantation home on the Waccamaw, near Murrells Inlet, he sat in her bedchamber, which remained just as she left it. In the shadowy room darkened by encroaching oaks, he grieved for his missing wife, and for their dead son.

In New York City, the dapper figure of an aging lawyer could be seen in the late afternoons making his way to the docks. Day after day for months he stood looking out to sea, awaiting the arrival of his beloved only daughter, Theodosia Burr Alston. If Aaron Burr had ever loved anyone besides himself, it was his daughter and her son.

Brookgreen Gardens includes Joseph's plantation, The Oaks, where he built a beautiful manor house for his bride, Theodosia. If her ghost walks the paths at Brookgreen or sighs in the winds around the great oaks, it is a troubled spirit, saddened by many events in her young life.

Born in 1783, Theodosia grew up in New York City. She was the only child of Aaron Burr, whom she idolized. Her mother, Theodosia Prevost Burr, died when the little girl was only nine. From that time on, her father considered her his hostess and housekeeper. She was his constant companion. Her father saw to it that she studied all subjects usually taught only to young men. She was proficient in several languages, art, music and history, and became one of the most educated and cultured young women in America.

Aaron Burr was a brilliant lawyer, a U. S. senator, and third vice-president, serving with President Thomas Jefferson. His enemies (and he had many) called him "an infamous rascal." Burr was ambitious for his own advancement, and many said he was unscrupulous as well.

Many visitors came to the Burr home in New York and to Richmond Hill, his estate near the city. One of the visitors was a wealthy young man from South Carolina, Joseph Alston, owner of The Oaks Plantation. He, too, was knowledgeable and well educated. He was drawn to Theodosia, who was the belle of New York society. She had many suitors, but soon had eyes for no one but Joseph.

From their first meeting they were infatuated with each other. He described his two-thousand-acre plantation as a lush semi-tropical paradise on a beautiful river near the Carolina coast. He forgot to mention the hot, humid summers, the unhealthy season on the plantations. Theodosia was entranced; they could scarcely wait to marry.

Her friends were dismayed. They could not understand how she could leave her home and position in New York to marry this brash, unknown young man from the South. Surprisingly, her father encouraged the marriage, and the whirlwind courtship continued.

On February 2, 1801, they were married in Albany. Lovely Theodosia was eighteen and Joseph was twenty-two. While on their honeymoon, they spent some time in the new capital city of Washington and attended the inauguration of Thomas Jefferson as president and Aaron Burr as vice-president. Then they sailed down the coast to Charleston and Georgetown.

The move introduced the lovely and cultured New York girl to a way of life so different that she might have been in another country. As mistress of a great rice plantation, which extended from the Waccamaw River to the Atlantic Ocean, she had many duties. She found herself responsible for the health and well-being of over two hundred slaves. The idea of slavery greatly disturbed Theodosia. It went against all her principles. In time, the slaves loved and respected her. They were a comfort in her times of need.

She was also responsible for the home, and for an elaborate social life which included frequent entertaining. Everyone from Murrells Inlet to Charleston wanted to see and meet the new bride. There were more invitations than the Alstons could possibly accept.

In addition, the heat and humidity of the Low Country summers and the strange fevers left Theodosia frail and sickly. She was scarcely able to cope with her responsibilities. She soon became pregnant, with more health problems. The Negro house servants petted her and cared for her like one of their children.

Letters from her father offered all kinds of advice and cheered her, especially when Joseph was away in Charleston or Columbia. Burr advised her to stay at Magnolia Beach (now Huntington Beach) on their property or go to the mountains to escape the heat. She followed his advice.

Her son was born early in 1802. She and Joseph named him Aaron Burr Alston, for his grandfather. He was a joy to everyone, especially his grandfather, who visited often. The house slaves adored him and he always had playmates. The only problem the family faced was Theodosia's frailty.

Serious trouble began for Aaron Burr in 1804. He shot and killed Alexander Hamilton in a duel. Public opinion turned against him. Although dueling was legal, Burr was threatened with a murder indictment. Theodosia grieved for her father, and for Hamilton's wife and children, whom she had known.

To add to Burr's mounting troubles, he became involved in 1806 in a land scheme along the Mississippi River. He and his partner, Harman Blennerhasset, were later accused of treason. It seems they were plotting to take over land west of the river and set up a new nation in the Louisiana Territory, just acquired from France. The two men were tried in federal court in Richmond, and acquitted. Theodosia went to Richmond to support her father. She sat beside him every day in court, convinced he could do no wrong.

Afterwards, Burr sailed for France, where he spent four years in self-imposed exile. He had lost his property, fortune, and most of his friends. Returning home in 1812, Burr found terrible news awaiting him in New York. His ten-year-old grandson had died of fever, and Joseph and Theodosia were inconsolable. They had buried their son in the family cemetery at The Oaks.

Joseph, newly elected governor of South Carolina, had many duties that kept him in Columbia. Although the War of 1812 against England had just started, he thought a visit with her father in New

York might help Theodosia deal with her grief and depression. Plans were made and Joseph accompanied her to Georgetown.

On December 31, 1812, Theodosia sailed from Georgetown on board *The Patriot* for the six-day voyage to New York. The small sailing vessel left the port and was never seen or heard from again.

As days and weeks passed with no word of *The Patriot,* frantic letters were exchanged by Joseph and Burr. The authorities searched shipping lanes and ports from New York to the Bahamas but found no evidence of the missing vessel. The worried father and husband of the lovely young woman had to live with the reality that she had disappeared.

The governor grieved for his wife and son until his untimely death in 1816, following a seizure. He was buried in the Alston family cemetery beside his small son.

Many theories have surfaced about the fate of *The Patriot.* Surely it could have sunk in a winter storm off Cape Hatteras, in the "Graveyard of the Atlantic." Piracy was rare in the 1800s, yet persistent rumors told of deathbed confessions by pirates of attacking the ship.

Or was *The Patriot* lured onto the rocks and shoals along the Outer Banks of North Carolina by "Bankers?" These heartless men lived by salvaging the cargo of wrecked ships.

In nearly two centuries no theory has yet been proven. Her disappearance remains a mystery. Many people have felt her presence along the walks at Brookgreen, or in the cemetery, or even along the beach, as she strives to join her beloved husband and dear little son.

Where, oh, where is Theodosia?

Entrance to the Alston family cemetery on The Oaks,
where Theodosia's husband and small son were buried
Courtesy of Barry McGee

13

A LIGHTED HOUSE AFLOAT

I saw a lighted house afloat,
I thought it was a ship.
If I knew how they did it,
I'd like to take a trip!

"I saw it!" the little boy said. "I tell you I saw it!" He was so excited that he could scarcely speak.

"And what did you see?" his father asked.

"I was walking on the beach a few blocks north of the Swash. I looked up and suddenly I saw a lighted house come sailing out of the Swash and on into the ocean."

"Well?" his father said. "A house? Not a fishing boat? Are you sure?"

"Of course I'm sure. I turned away to see if anyone else was on the beach, and when I looked again, the house had vanished!" The boy kicked his toe in the sand. "Did you ever see such a thing, Dad?"

"Not really, although I've often looked for it."

The boy's eyes glowed with excitement. His dad understood! He believed him! "Tell me about it, Dad, please!"

The two, father and son, settled themselves against a high sand dune, where they were sheltered from the freakish autumn winds. "It's a long story. Are you sure you want to hear it?"

The boy's expression was all the answer the man needed. And so he began a tale lost in the shadows of the past.

*   *   *

For as long as anyone remembers, this run of water has been known as "Withers Swash." It lies along Third Avenue South, flowing into the great Atlantic Ocean on a stretch of strand known to old-timers as "Spivey Beach." A swash is a narrow inlet through which high tides rush inland and low tides ebb out to sea.

In 1780, near the end of the Revolution, widow Mary Esther Withers moved from her prosperous Maryville Plantation, south of Georgetown, to Long Bay on the Grand Strand. Her husband, before his death, had received grants of land for thousands of acres near Georgetown and along the Grand Strand.

Mary and her three sons, Francis, Richard and Robert, hoped to escape marauding British soldiers who had occupied Georgetown since the early days of fighting. The sons were not too happy about leaving all their social activities and friends in Georgetown, but they soon settled down and tried to raise rice and indigo on newly cleared land prepared by slaves. Producing naval stores and timber proved more lucrative. They also spent more time on their plantation near Georgetown and enjoyed the leisurely life of wealthy planters.

In 1801 Mary Withers died, and her sons buried her in the churchyard of Prince George Winyah Episcopal Church in Georgetown. Her gravestone stands near the door that opens into the cemetery. The town of Maryville, across the Sampit River, was named for her plantation.

In the late 1700s, Francis Withers had decided to build a big plantation house for his family on "a bold bluff overlooking the swash." That bluff, somewhat weathered and worn down, can be viewed from a parking lot north of Fifth Avenue South. The house faced the beautiful lake, which drained into the swash. Fields south and west of the house were planted in cotton, with a small patch of indigo. Voluntary indigo plants still appear today, from time to time, descendants of seeds planted two centuries ago.

The family enjoyed the cool breezes and clear waters of their lake. As the years went by, Francis Withers and several other members of the family were buried in Withers Cemetery, located on First Avenue and Collins Street. It is across the lake from where the big house stood. The cemetery is still used by several local families.

Unfortunately, the Withers home no longer exists. In 1822 one of the most violent hurricanes to ever strike the mainland of North America came ashore along the Grand Strand. It hit the coast after three days of heavy rains, and the storm surge coincided with the high tide. The water rushed in through Withers Swash and into the lake. Hurricane force winds continued to blow walls of water inland, battering trees, crops, sheds and stables.

The beautiful Withers House stood a little higher on its hill. It seemed to be the safest place around. Eighteen family members and neighbors took refuge on the upper floor and lighted candles and lamps. As frightened as they were, the atmosphere was almost like a party, as they ate and drank and took comfort in being together. But not for long.

According to *The Independent Republic: A Survey of History of Horry County, South Carolina*, a sudden surge of water struck the lake. It reached the foundation of the great house. An engulfing wave beat against the house, lifting it off its foundation. As the doomed inmates of the house prayed and held on to each other, they felt the structure lifted up as it floated across the lake and down the channel of the swash, into the vast heaving ocean. Their moans and cries were lifted to the heavens as they realized their plight.

The windows shone brightly from the lamps and candles inside as the house sailed away, looking like a ship setting out on a voyage.

But only for a few minutes.

Reportedly, the force of the wind and waves of water, pushed inland by the raging tide, crushed the house and broke it apart. All eighteen people in the house lost their lives.

A little-known legend says that on wild stormy nights, the big house can sometimes be seen floating down the swash and out to sea.

*   *   *

"My friends and I used to watch for hours, trying to see the house," the father told his eager son. "They say October might be the best month for viewing. It's the time for 'hants' and 'specters' and all kinds of eerie phenomena. We'll try it sometime."

*   *   *

Understandably, the rest of the Withers family in Georgetown abandoned their land holdings, which were later sold to Joshua John Ward. The large acreage included most of what is now Myrtle Beach. The house was gone—and the fields grew up in pines and scrub oaks.

However, the Withers name was not forgotten. It is used for a street, a cemetery, for Withers Big Swamp, and for Withers 8-mile Swamp, which extends across the Waterway toward Socastee.

On April 30, 1888, the first Grand Strand area post office opened, located near the swash. It was called Withers, South Carolina. It served fishermen and farmers along the road to Socastee. Daniel "Dinkins" Cox served as the first postmaster.

With the building of the railroad to the beach, Myrtle Beach Post Office opened May 21, 1901. Withers Post Office closed in September 1901.

On December 16, 1996, the Withers Swash Boardwalk Dedication and Ribbon Cutting was held. The ceremony was a triumph for those who have worked for the improvement of the ecology of all swashes and inlets. Road building, homes ringing the lake and swash, and storm water run-off over many years have contaminated the once pure and clear waters. Hopefully, this condition is now improving.

The loss of the great Withers house and the loss of so many lives swept out to sea cannot be forgotten. Behind every name lies a story, especially when lives are lost tragically. Surely those spirits try to bring a message over the years. There are those who have reported a glimpse of the lighted house afloat.

Look for it, on a dreary, stormy night, when the trees drip tears of light rain and fog, when tall grasses and shrubs writhe in the grip of gusts of wind, when sorrowful voices are part of the wind sound.

It is a proper setting for ghosts to walk, for the spirits to return, and for a lighted house to float out to sea.

14

THE CAROLINA BAYS

They call them "bays," these oval lakes along the Coastal Plain of Horry County. It is interesting to see them from the air or from the high causeway and bridges of Highway 22, as road construction continues. Some of the lakes have been drained and filled as housing projects are built. Others are used as part of the landscaping.

Geologists have studied the formation of the mysterious bays. One theory states that giant meteor showers ages ago may have caused the oval depressions. Some of them gradually filled with fresh water and became lakes. Another theory claims these were sink holes above underground rivers and that seeping water gradually filled them. Other depressions, rimmed in white sand, were filled with thickets of ferns, bushes and trees.

The American Sweet Bay Tree still flourishes near the bays, filling the air with its delightful perfume in season. The tree is classified as Magnolia virginiana. Other unusual plants have been observed and classified by naturalists: the rare Venus Flytrap, pink dogwood, yellow jessamine, pitcher plants and numerous native bushes and trees. In the past, the bays have been an area of deep swamps and lagoon-like lakes. For centuries they have been the natural habitat of an endless variety of birds and animals.

Early settlers found the thick native growth around the bays almost impenetrable. They were the home of the white-tail deer, black bears and wildcats. Alligators flailed the waters and many snakes slithered through the undergrowth. Children were warned by cautious mothers: "Don't go in the woods alone!" It was dangerous, as everyone knew.

The bays have always been places of mystery and wonder. Patches of quicksand added to the danger of wandering around in the thickets.

Many difficulties were encountered by crews building the railroad from Conway to Myrtle Beach in 1900. Highway 501, which parallels the railroad for most of the way, had a host of problems. The road was begun in the late 1930s, put on hold during World War II, and finally finished and paved by 1948. It cut the distance to Conway nearly in half. During construction, several pieces of equipment vanished in pits of quicksand, but modern technology prevailed and the road was completed.

Unwary hunters and fishermen, wandering through the bays alone, have encountered dangers and sometimes lost their lives. It was easy to lose your way, especially at night. Animals prowling the dark woods were on the lookout for prey of all kinds. Black bears require a large area to roam in search of food. Unfortunate ones have crossed the Waterway into Myrtle Beach, where they were captured.

The first invaders of the Carolina Bays from Conway were men who came with buckets to scrape sap or gum from the beautiful longleaf pines, for making naval stores (tar and pitch for ship building). Then came the lumbermen, setting up sawmills and clear-cutting an area, before moving on. The new era has brought roads and housing developments. Startled deer and puzzled bears have no place to go. Rare plants and small animals are being destroyed, once again, in the name of progress.

From time to time forest fires have invaded the bays. Recently extensive fires have burned hundreds of acres of forests and thickets, and threatened some homes.

The Carolina Bays are fast disappearing.

Three centuries ago, sailing ships often came in close to shore looking for an inlet or swash to enter. The crew could see the lush growth back of the beautiful white sandy beaches. They were sometimes fooled by its appearance. Going ashore into the jungle-like woods was not as safe as it looked.

The story is told of Captain George Lowther, a pirate from London, England. He sailed as second mate on the *Gambia Castle*, a trading vessel. Seizing the opportunity, he led a successful mutiny and renamed the ship *The Happy Delivery*. Since they were already in trouble with the authorities, most of the crew went along with the idea of piracy. For a time they were quite busy, assembling a small fleet from ships they had captured. They spread fear wherever they appeared, showing no mercy for their victims.

Right off the South Carolina coast, Captain Lowther ordered his men to attack an English ship. He followed the usual plan of flying the English flag until he was close to the other ship. Then he displayed his Jolly Roger flag and the battle began. He was sure his surprise attack would end in victory, but the English ship maneuvered Lowther too close to shore, and his ship stuck on a sandbar. To avoid capture, Lowther abandoned his ship and crew. It was a cowardly thing to do.

He swam ashore and fled into the thicket, frantically trying to save himself from the gallows. Farther and farther he scrambled into the jungle-like growth. No one would try to follow into such a tangle of bushes and trees, overgrown with vines.

Without food or safe water, Lowther could not survive long. He found no house or human in the forest, and he had no idea which way to go. At night he cowered in fear, trying to find a safe place to sleep among the bushes. Bears or wildcats often circled the spot where he tried to hide. He lived in fear; his hunger and misery increased. His trick of fleeing into the woods had backfired on him.

Months later, a group of hunters discovered part of a skeleton underneath thick bushes with a small pistol by its side. The decayed body had been attacked by animals. Cause of death was reported as a suicide. The pirate who had lived by the sword had died by his own hand. Does his troubled spirit still wander through the bays?

Captain William Lewis is reported to have pursued his career of piracy from 1717 to 1726. Up and down the Carolina coast, from Charleston to Wilmington, he captured several trading vessels. At the same time, he was so cruel and evil to his own crew that they finally murdered him in his sleep. The superstitious pirates felt that anyone so depraved must be in league with the devil himself.

They threw Lewis' body overboard and left it to wash up on the beach, then sailed away as quickly as possible, because they were afraid his spirit might follow them. Some say his spirit still walks the beach, vowing vengeance on his crew. Perhaps he appears on dark, stormy nights, his angry cries mingling with the thunder and wind.

Many pirates met their death or were captured along the Carolina coast. Numbers of hunters and fishermen vanished into the bays and were never heard from again. Surely their restless spirits still wander along the beaches or in the mystery-shrouded bays.

15

THE GRAY MAN

The Gray Man remains unchallenged as South Carolina's most famous ghost. For generations, children of the Palmetto State have grown up hearing about the friendly but somber warnings of the Gray Man of Pawleys Island. Even so, it is a mystifying story of a ghost who is not scary or fearful. Instead his mission seems to be to help people, to save lives when he appears. Somehow it's out of character for a ghost.

Nell Graydon, in her book *Carolina Ghosts*, said there are at least a half-dozen different stories of the identity of the Gray Man. In each case, he comes through as a helpful ghost whose aim is to warn people of impending disaster in a storm. Many instances of his warnings have been cited over the years.

In 1993 the story appeared on a television show, *Unsolved Mysteries*, filmed at Pawleys Island. It featured a Pawleys Island couple who claimed the Gray Man's warning spared their lives and home in 1989 during Hurricane Hugo.

The legend has continued for almost two centuries. A favorite version of the Gray Man's beginnings is a romantic tale of undying love, dating back to 1822.

Early in September of that year, travelers saw a handsome young man riding atop a galloping horse, along the sandy, rutted road that led from the mainland to Pawleys Island. His manservant rode a horse beside him, having accompanied him from Charleston. The young man had just returned from a two-year stay in Europe. After completing his education, he had made the "Grand Tour" of several countries before returning to begin his law practice in Charleston. It was customary training for the young, aristocratic men of the South.

Now thoughts of his lovely fiancée filled the young man's mind. He was going to visit her at her father's beach house on Pawleys Island. In his absence she had made plans for their wedding. Their letters had gone back and forth during their long separation. It would be a joyous reunion.

Meanwhile, his fiancée had received notice of his visit. Her impatience and eagerness mounted as time went by. She had sent out the invitations for an elaborate wedding at the local Episcopal church. By all signs, it would be a great occasion. If only he would come!

Joyfully, the young man hastened to the island. He was having so much fun that he challenged his servant to a race. Faster and faster they went. The young man veered onto a side trail, thinking it was a shortcut. Unfortunately the path led to a marshy bog, an innocent looking area of coastal quicksand, deceptive and deadly.

Suddenly the speeding horse stumbled and fell, pitching his rider into the mire. The young man struggled desperately, his head and face submerged in the strangling quicksand. Try as he might, the servant could not save him. The horse and young man were sucked under, leaving no trace on the smooth surface of the bog.

The family at the beach house heard a heavy knock on the door. It was the servant, with heartbreaking news for the young woman. When she understood what had happened, she collapsed. She lay in bed for days, uncaring for the advice of her distraught father. She preferred to be alone in her sorrow.

Finally the girl's parents, fearing for her health and sanity, insisted that she join the family for meals and other activities. To please them, she began taking walks along the beach in the late afternoons. Her slight figure cast a pallid silhouette in the evening gloom.

Late one overcast afternoon, just as night began to fall, the girl walked alone through a misty fog that curled in from the water. Suddenly she saw a man, dressed in gray, moving over the beach toward her. As the mist thickened between them, she thought she recognized her dead lover. The girl raced desperately toward him. Perhaps the servant was wrong and he had somehow escaped from the quicksand.

The man did not speak. Instead he repeatedly gestured toward the mainland. Without warning he vanished in the swirling fog and darkness.

When the girl finally slept that night, she dreamed of a terrible storm sweeping toward the island. The next day she told her father about the Gray Man on the beach who seemed to be warning her, and of the violent storm in her dreams. Her father paid little attention to her wild tales. He feared his daughter was losing her mind, and decided she must immediately see a doctor in Charleston.

Soon after the family left Pawleys Island, the Hurricane of 1822 struck the coast. It was one of the worst storms ever recorded along the Atlantic Coast. It resulted in great loss of life and property. Homes were wrenched from their foundations and splintered; the remnants and trash floated out to sea.

The girl, her father and family journeyed safely to Charleston. When they returned to the island, their home was unharmed in the midst of the destruction. Others told later of having seen a man, dressed in gray, coming ashore out of the storm, and then disappearing.

And so the legend grew—if you saw the Gray Man and heeded his warning to leave, you might survive a storm unharmed.

The Gray Man
Courtesy of Harry Tomlinson, Alpha Media Creations, Inc.

The Gray Man has given warning many times since 1822. Everyone who sees him gives the same description: a shrouded, grayish figure, usually along the beach, sometimes coming out of the water. One woman told of bringing her grandchildren to her Pawleys Island house for a brief vacation. A day or so later she saw a man answering the Gray Man's description walking along the water's edge. As she watched, he became less distinct, and finally she saw only a blur. She left as a storm began, which produced drastic flooding of low-lying areas. She and the children were safe. Later she found her house unharmed by the storm.

In 1954, before Hurricane Hazel, a Georgetown automobile dealer who lived on the island told of seeing the Gray Man. The man said he walked out to a lookout deck atop the high dunes to look at the rolling surf. As he stood there, he glimpsed a lone figure moving along the water's edge. He identified the figure as a man, dressed in old fashioned clothes–the Gray Man. When he tried to call out to him, the figure vanished. The automobile dealer left the island in time to avoid the hurricane.

Several years ago a violent storm struck Pawleys Island and the Carolina coast. Two men riding in a car during the storm wondered what they should do.

One man said, "We sure need the Gray Man to tell us whether or not we should leave."

The other man responded quickly, "Well, there he is up ahead! Why don't you ask him?"

And it was! They saw the figure of a man, dressed all in gray, his shoulders hunched up against the driving wind and rain, while he strode purposefully along the island road. They stopped the car near the man.

"Sir, are you the Gray Man?" one of them asked out the window.

"No!" the man exploded. His head bent against the rain

The men in the car were disappointed. One said, "I'm sorry, sir. You're dressed all in gray and out in this storm. No offense, sir." They started to drive on.

"Look," the man in the storm said, "I had a heart attack, and my doctor told me I had to exercise. So I'm going to exercise if it kills me!" And he plodded on.

The man was wearing a dull gray, knitted warm-up suit, with the hood pulled over his head.

Today we depend on the Weather Bureau for warnings, watches, and evacuation notices in the face of a threatening hurricane or coastal storm. Certainly you should heed these warnings. But if you happen to see the Gray Man–take his advice and leave quickly!

16

THE LIGHTHOUSE KEEPER'S DAUGHTER

Wild, beautiful North Island dominates the entrance to Winyah Bay. Wind-swept and storm-lashed, this island takes the brunt of Atlantic storms and the ocean's high tides. It forms a protective barrier for the channel and the Winyah Bay harbor.

Along the east side lie sandy deserted beaches, accessible only by boat. They are inhabited by skittish shore birds, turtles and crabs, ambling awkwardly along at their own pace. Cedars, pines, palmettos and oaks, gnarled and twisted by storm winds into fantasy shapes, mass together as another barrier. At the southern tip of the island, piles of rocks, called North Jetty and South Jetty, protect the entrance to the main channel.

On the western side of the island, a crisscross of narrow, uncharted channels divide the low marshy land into isles that may disappear with any high tide. This boggy sunken land forms an unexcelled wildlife haven. Visitors must approach by boat, since there are no roads or bridges. Patches of quicksand abound and can catch anyone unawares, even a president of the United States. President Grover Cleveland learned that on a hunting trip in December 1894.

Across Mud Bay, tiny Pumpkinseed Island, Marsh Island and Big Marsh Island appear. Goat Island, creeks and marshes lead north to Debidue Island. All of it makes a natural fantasy land.

This is North Island, lovely and wind-swept in its near-tropical setting. It has been the scene of many events, some scarcely noted by historians. The island might have been the site of the failed 1526 Spanish settlement. Bloodthirsty pirates found rest and relaxation ashore, as well as fresh water and food. During the Revolution, in the late 1770's, the Frenchman, Marquis de Lafayette, landed on North Island with a party of his men. His ship had been blown off course. He was anxious to reach Philadelphia and offer his help to General Washington and the Patriots. His group received horses and journeyed overland.

Before the days of official weather forecasters, ships' captains looked for signs in nature and followed their instincts about the safety of sailing. Such skills were life-saving necessities. On rocky coasts and hazardous reefs, lighthouses were built to point the way for ships to navigate.

As shipping into Winyah Bay and Georgetown increased, a lighthouse was erected on the southern tip of North Island. A thick stone building, it had a great whale-oil lantern on top. It had to be kept burning on foggy, dark days, and it always shone brightly at night. It was a reliable sign and trusted by all sailors.

A lighthouse keeper in the early 1800s lived there with his small, fair-haired daughter. Her mother had died at her birth, and she and her father were very close. She considered herself her father's helper. Their cozy living quarters, nestled beside the tower, provided a happy home for the two of them. She loved to hear the fog horn sound at regular intervals in stormy weather.

Two or three times a month, the captain and his daughter made the trip to Georgetown to buy necessary supplies. The little girl, named Annie, always looked forward to these excursions. She enjoyed seeing the people and shops in the bustling bayside town. Annie helped her father choose their supplies, and he rewarded her with a treat of candy.

Annie's father scheduled their trips into town carefully with the tides and weather. It was important to see that the great light was burning before darkness fell. They went in to town in a small boat on the incoming tide, and returned on the ebbing tide. The father eyed the skies and clouds to be sure no storm was in the offing.

One day they set out for a special trip to town, with Annie so excited she could scarcely sit still. After their shopping, they ate, walked around the streets, and enjoyed the day. The captain loaded the small boat carefully. They climbed aboard, waving to people on the dock, and set out across the bay and channel.

Before long Annie and the captain noticed a brisk wind blowing and ominous clouds gathering overhead. Heavy rain and hail began to fall, swamping the little boat. It began to sink.

Desperately the captain tied his little daughter to his back and tried to swim through the tall waves and dangerous seas. It was an impossible undertaking. Again and again the two of them went underwater, but the father kept swimming. Later, he could not recall crawling ashore. He lay there in shock and exhaustion.

When he became fully conscious, he called to Annie, but she did not respond. To his horror he found his little daughter, still strapped to his back, drowned. The father never recovered from his loss. He wandered the streets of Georgetown, disoriented, calling for Annie.

And Annie never rested in her small grave. Time and again, she has been seen, warning shrimp boats and other ships' pilots of a sudden violent coastal storm. A sweet, fair-haired little girl appears to someone on a boat. She points to the calm waters and says, "Go back!" It is a warning to obey, as many have learned. It means, "A storm is coming!"

Newcomers scoff. "A ghost child? Here in Georgetown?" But when they hear the story, they are more open to the idea.

If Annie should appear, please heed her warning. It could save your life.

17

THE WITCH'S CURSE

It had to be a flaw in the slab of granite—or was it? How could a curse from the 1700s, uttered by a woman about to die, have such an effect on Colonel Jonathan Buck's monument?

As our tour bus traveled through Bucksport, Maine, the guide told a haunting story, remembered and repeated for many generations in the New England town. Our interest was keen for we were all familiar with Bucksport and Bucksville, on the Waccamaw River in Horry County, South Carolina. These river villages were settled in the early 1800s by descendants of Colonel Buck of Bucksport, Maine.

It seems that Colonel Buck was an outstanding leader and founder of the town, which was named for him. He also served as judge of the local court. Long after his death, there appeared a rumor, which became a legend.

As usual, there are several different versions of the legend, told by many different writers. Yet the story became well-known because of these writings. In 1942 the town published a booklet for the one hundredth anniversary of the founding of Bucksport, with a chapter entitled, "Legends of the Buck Monument." The Reverend A. G. Hempstead, Pastor of Franklin Street Methodist Church, Bucksport, had researched the legends and contributed a chapter to the booklet.

According to Reverend Hempstead, Colonel Buck, a strong Methodist, was almost Puritanical in his hatred of witchcraft. Born in Massachusetts in 1719, he heard tales as a small child of the Salem Witch Trials. Twenty "witches" were hanged in Salem in 1692 and two more died in the prison there. They were convicted on scant evidence. It was a terror-filled period, a blight on colonial history.

In 1764 Colonel Buck moved his family to land he had surveyed on the Penobscot River in Maine. He encouraged others to come and founded the small town of Bucksport. In time he served as Provincial Agent, Colonel of Militia, and Justice of the Peace. Yet he is not remembered for all of these worthy achievements.

Instead a flawed piece of granite has caused legends to swirl around his monument in the cemetery, casting spurious doubts on his honorable reputation.

Colonel Buck died in 1795 and was buried beside his wife, who had died in 1789. A modest slate headstone marked his grave. Some years later, family members erected a fifteen-foot granite marker near the grave in his honor. The monument became a landmark for Bucksport. It stands just inside a wrought-iron fence, in a cemetery which is located on Bucksport's main thoroughfare, State Route 15 and U. S. Highway 1, directly south of Bangor, and a widely-used route.

Old Maine, with its myriad inlets and river mouths, was the historic site of many small settlements. There are numerous haunted places along the coast. Fog and mist settling over little towns may cause some of the reported sightings of otherworldly figures, but believers cling to their stories.

Colonel Buck's prominent marker was viewed by many people. Some of them began to notice the gradual appearance of a shape, or marking, directly beneath the name "Buck." As the mark became more distinct, anyone could see a leg and foot, perhaps encased in a stocking. The rumors began. Had the honorable Colonel antagonized someone who then vowed to haunt him? Had this "pillar of the community" been involved with another woman? Had he committed a crime that had never come to light?

Many people came to look, to mutter and shake their heads.

Embarrassed family members had the granite slab cleaned and sanded and polished several times. Each time the leg reappeared, and more tales were told.

One story appeared in 1902 called "The Witch's Curse, a Legend of An Old Maine Town," by J. O. Whittemore. It scandalized local people but became popular as many heard it or read about it. The story brought an endless line of sightseers, filled with avid curiosity about the monument, to Bucksport.

Many years earlier, Colonel Buck had considered the practice of witchcraft and vowed it would never appear in his town, as it did sporadically in New England. Though hard to prove, the charge of being a witch had ruined many lives. Judge Buck decided to purge his town, as an example to others.

An old woman named Ida Black lived in a rundown hut on the edge of Bucksport. She was feeble and frail and wore ragged clothing, all of black. Furthermore, she mumbled to herself, or to the devil. Who knew? Young girls tagged after her, teasing and calling her names. It was all Buck needed. The senile old woman, with no one to care what happened to her, was accused of witchcraft and brought to trial.

Judge Buck, presiding at Ida Black's trial, listened to the scant evidence that the few witnesses presented. It is said that he took little time to consider the testimony, but quickly pronounced the old woman guilty of being a witch and consorting with the devil. Ida

Black stood alone before the judge, mumbling to herself, as he condemned her to death by hanging. The harsh sentence surprised the people of Bucksport, who whispered and wondered at its severity.

Ida Black scarcely knew what was happening until the day of the hanging. Then she pled with the judge to spare her life. When he ignored her, she cursed him and promised that her foot would appear on his stone. Seemingly it did, some years after Buck's death.

The story has been told many times, with several variations: a curse from the grave of a poor old woman, accusing her judge of wrongdoing.

The Buck family monument in Bucksport Cemetery is considered "one of the most remarkable and curious objects in the State of Maine." Of course, it is not unusual for a flaw in granite to take a recognizable shape. But the story of the "witch's curse" and the appearance of the foot and leg under Buck's name have combined to make a local legend.

Three decades later and a thousand miles south of Bucksport, Maine, Judge Buck's grandson came to Coastal South Carolina to seek his fortune. Captain Henry Buck arrived in Georgetown in 1828, and settled about thirty-five miles north along the Waccamaw River. The attraction was the plentiful supply of lumber from forests of tall pine trees.

Over the next hundred years, three towns, established by the Buck family, grew up quickly along the wide river. Bucksville, Bucksport, and Port Harrellson were lumber mill settlements. Men came to work and brought their families, which called for houses, stores, schools, churches, and doctors and lawyers. By 1930, they were abandoned ghost towns; the forests were "cut out," some buildings burned down, and people had moved on to find other homes and jobs. The Great Depression was setting in across the

The Buck Monument, with the woman's leg and foot
Courtesy of the Bucksport, Maine Chamber of Commerce

nation and the world. The economic outlook seemed drab and gray everywhere.

Had the witch's curse reached out across a hundred years and a thousand miles to destroy the success of Judge Jonathan Buck's descendants? It was something for Buck family members to think about privately. Theirs had been a tremendous empire.

Bucksville once rivaled Conway, with its lumber, naval stores, and shipbuilding. Today all that remains of the original town is the Buck home on the river, which is listed in *The National Register of Historic Places*. It is the home of another Henry Buck, great-grandson of the founder. Nearby stands Hebron United Methodist Church, built by ships' carpenters. It is still in use, and the Buck family cemetery across the narrow road is the resting place used by descendants. Many fine homes have been built in recent years along the river by Horry County natives.

Bucksport, farther down the river, still has a picturesque river harbor, used by boats of all kinds. It is the location where the Inland Waterway, built in 1936, joins the Waccamaw and flows on to Winyah Bay at Georgetown. The derelict remains of a beautiful old house, built before 1850, stands in ruins. The sparse population lives close to Highway 701. It no longer has stores and a post office.

Does Ida Black's curse live on, in these Waccamaw River ghost towns?

18

ROAD'S END PLANTATION HOUSE

> Candlelight in the attic
> A footstep on the stair
> Soft laughter in the parlor
> And yet—no one is there.

Scattered around Horry County are many old houses of note; each of them has a story of generations to tell. Road's End Plantation House is one of these. People who lived along the road called it "the mansion," and the resident families were "the rich folks."

U. S. Highway 701 connects Conway and Georgetown and parallels the Waccamaw River. On Highway 48, near the waterfront, Road's End House sits in desolate splendor. It has a splendid view of the river, but there is no one to enjoy it. The lumbermen or plantation owners and their ladies have been long gone—only their spirits remain.

Viewed from a distance, the house has the look of New England cottages along the shore. The Cape Cod-style building had outer walls of cypress shingles, now gray tinged with green. Its steep roof was built to help heavy snows (that never came) to slide away.

The classic building has been vacant for nearly half a century, since the 1950s. The house has slowly deteriorated, with broken windows and holes in the roof. The upstairs rooms are inaccessible. Yet the style and dignity of the design are apparent after more than a century and a half. Massive oak trees enfold and guard the house.

Road's End, formerly called Bucksport Plantation House, was built by Jonathan Buck II. He was the son of Henry Buck and the grandson of Jonathan Buck, Sr. of Bucksport, Maine. Henry Buck came south to find lumber and naval stores for the family shipbuilding industry in Maine. The Bucks established three mills to produce and ship the valuable lumber. Settlements grew into villages, as long as the lumbering continued. Unfortunately, when the mills left for other areas, some of the settlements became ghost towns.

Mr. and Mrs. Donald V. Richardson, Sr. bought the property in the early 1900s to be their home. They developed the Bucksport Marina, after the Intracoastal Waterway and Waccamaw River merged in 1936. Pleasure boating became much more important.

By 1954 Road's End stood empty. As the years went by, no one came and other residents watched and waited. The house became a place to avoid, almost a place of fear. Children peeped fearfully toward the attic, where lights sometimes appeared. Were they candles from the past, or reflections of starlight through the broken roof? The lonely hoot of an owl, disturbed in his tree, would scatter the children as they ran. Often they heard sounds in the house, thumping or walking. But only ghostly feet could walk on those broken floors or stairs. Of course, animals could get in the house, but the ghostly explanation was more interesting. Was it the keening wind, or was it voices and laughter from long-departed souls?

And so generations of children watch and wonder. It is a place of mystery, this old house, a place to avoid, yet it interests people. Why was it left empty for so many years? It was so beautiful in the early years, a mansion for all to see, and for rich folks to enjoy.

Now the house stands waiting, its splendor dimmed by the passing of the years, its occupants the memories and spirits of the past.

19

"OVER THE RIVER..."

"Over the River" truly described the terrain and way of travel in Horry County before the 1900s. The Waccamaw River was wide and deep. Its strong currents rushed toward the Atlantic Ocean at Georgetown. The river was often "in freshet," as President George Washington noted in his journal, and overflowed its banks. Everywhere there were streams, creeks, and swamps, handicapping the traveler.

Shallow streams could be forded by horse and buggy or wagon, but they were sometimes treacherous. Farmers cut lengths of logs and laid them in muddy or swampy places to keep from getting stuck in the mud; this was called a "corduroy road." It was a bumpy, hard way to travel. Then too, quicksand abounded in the bays and swamps near the coast. The thickets and forests of pine, cedar, holly, oak, yaupon, swamp magnolia and myrtle had long been the habitat of black bears, wildcats, and deer.

In the coastal streams, the warning was: "Watch out for alligators!" Travelers found danger everywhere.

For settlers across the Waccamaw, travel to Kingston (Conway) for necessary business was difficult. One man wanted to be buried in a Christian cemetery in the town, not "under a tree in the wilderness." When he died, his sons fashioned his wooden coffin, loaded it on their flat ferry, and headed across the river. Unfortunately the strong current of the river caused the ferry to tilt, and the coffin slid into the water. The harried sons towed the coffin beside the ferry to the bank.

Hiring a horse and wagon, the sons took their father into town and to the graveyard, where he had a proper (somewhat wet) burial. Coffins were prone to slide, and this happened several times before adequate cemeteries were opened "across the river."

Ferries were usually operated by families. As many as sixteen were in operation in the late 1800s, from the North Carolina line to Georgetown. A few were still in use in 1930. Most of them had names from their locations or for the families operating them. Some names were: Star Bluff, Red Bluff, Bear Bluff, Cox's Ferry and Peach

The Waccamaw River
Courtesy of Barry McGee

Tree Ferry. Many of the great old plantations along the river had their own ferry.

The first ferries were shallow rafts, depending on long poles and muscle power. Methodist Bishop Francis Asbury, in 1801, was surprised to see women "poling" Hemingway's Ferry while their men did farm work.

Later the state licensed some of the ferries. Cable and pulley ferries replaced the pole-operated flats. If the ferryman happened to be on the other side of the river or asleep, you banged a plowshare against a piece of metal nailed on a tree until he came.

With no bridges before the early 1900s, people lived in close communities, and they seldom traveled far. Many in Horry County lived and worked and died in the same house and community where they were born.

The Waccamaw is still a scenic river of great beauty, especially along the River Walk in Conway. It gently winds its way past old lumber mills, little ghost towns, abandoned rice fields and fine old plantation homes to Winyah Bay and the Atlantic Ocean. With all its winding and twisting, the river stretches 150 miles from Lake Waccamaw, in North Carolina, to the Atlantic.

And now, it is night along the river, darkest night. Massive cyprus trees, growing in the water on either side, enclose the main stream. Tree branches overhead shut out faint star light. You are in a boat, and alone with the river. The water, with the tannic acid from oaks and cyprus trees, is as dark as the night. Someone said the water is the color of over-steeped tea.

At first it is a silent world, but as you wait, forest noises fill the air around you. You hunker down in your boat, glancing over your shoulder. A spiral of mist hovers above the water, and suddenly lifts into the air. Is it the spirit of a lost one? From earliest times, many people have lost their lives on the river. Treacherous currents have overturned boats and flats. Some bodies have been swept out to sea and never found.

One Conway man decided to go fishing, alone on the river, in his small boat. When he was told that it was too cold, he said he liked frosty weather–it was invigorating. So he went in the early part of a very cold day. Somehow he fell into the water, and, pulled by the current, drifted away from his boat. Hypothermia set in; the river claimed another victim.

Skiing is a favorite sport in summer. Numerous accidents have occurred and lives have been lost.

Some sections of the river remain primitive, a semi-tropical jungle of impenetrable growth, with nowhere to go ashore. Wild animals cry out in the night; there are still bears, wildcats, and alligators in and around the waters. The tale is told of a pirate who swam ashore, rather than be captured and hanged. He thrashed his way to the river–and he was never seen again.

The spirits of those who have lost their lives in the river over the centuries float in the glimmering mist.

20

THE GHOSTS OF OLD GUNN CHURCH

Anyone who has visited Old Gunn Church seems somewhat reluctant to go again, especially at Halloween or on any dark night.

There is an eerie fascination with the old church ruins for those who visit. Its name was Prince Frederick's Episcopal Church, Pee Dee, but it is better known as Old Gunn Church–named for the architect who fell to his death from the steep roof.

Only the massive, crumbling bell tower, standing tall against the sky, remains of the once lovely Gothic structure. The encroaching pines and white grave markers form a background for the clearing around the church. The tower looks like a lonely keep, a watchtower near the entrance to a great estate in England.

The old church was in disrepair for many years before it burned. It stood, empty and abandoned, with its pews and other furnishings taken away. Year after year, stormy winds and rain blew through broken windows and doors. It was a sad demise for the elaborate house of worship.

The ruins of the church are located on Plantersville Road, off Highway 701 between Conway and Georgetown. The name of the road came from the rich plantations that stretched for miles along the banks of the Pee Dee and Black Rivers. Nightingale, Arundel, Dirleton, Chicora Wood, Keithfield and many other plantations used

The remains of Old Gunn Church
Courtesy of J. K. Floyd

the rivers for travel and for watering the rice fields. The community of planters was the center of Prince Frederick's Parish, established in 1734.

For the convenience of the planters, a new church was commissioned, and construction began in 1859. The Episcopalian "rice barons" were a wealthy, close-knit society. The new building would reflect the culture and rich lifestyle of the Plantation South, and only the finest materials would be used. The builders chose to purchase these in England and have them shipped to Georgetown. Unfortunately the Union coastal blockade of the South during the Civil War halted the delivery of all imports.

Work had already begun on the church, and went on despite the blockade. The builders used the materials they had in hand. The brick and plaster structure they built promised to be stately and majestic, its beauty surpassing any building nearby. People came to watch as the Gothic-style bell tower took shape and rose above the treetops. Work on the tower came to an abrupt halt when the chief architect, Mr. Gunn, slipped and plummeted to his death from the slick tiled roof. The workers and everyone close by heard his horrible scream as he fell.

Some workers refused to continue constructing the tower; they insisted the place was haunted. The lack of materials and workers caused the unfinished church to be abandoned. It was left to the mercy of the elements during the war years and the decade that followed. The devastation of the war left no money to buy materials. Some of the fine old plantations had to be sold and divided, and people began to move away. It was the end of a distinctive way of life in the South.

Eventually other congregations donated money to complete the work on the church. Northern investors began to buy some of the property on the old plantations. When the church was completed in 1877, it drew a host of worshipers. A fine choir was organized, and the members came to practice almost every night at dusk. Strains of organ music lifted on the winds that stirred the trees. Carriages stopped along the road to listen to the lovely sounds. Often people wandered through the cemetery as they listened.

Some say the choir still sings. Their voices and the notes of the organ mingle with the wind and night sounds of the deserted church yard.

With changing times in the late 1800s, the depressed postwar economy worsened. Some members moved to Georgetown or Charleston to find jobs. Homes were abandoned or sold. As the congregation dwindled, services were held occasionally, then on special dates, and finally ceased.

Tales about the church and the death of its architect continued to be told. People in the community repeated the story to newcomers. Over the years, visitors have reported many strange and unexplained occurrences—lights in the upper tower (which is inaccessible), and moaning, shrieking or singing sounds. And worst of all, the horrible scream attributed to the architect, Mr. Gunn, as he fell to his death.

Each year at Halloween, carloads of young people make a pilgrimage to the ruins for the sole purpose of being frightened. The ancient encircling graveyard, the swaying trees, ragged bushes and tall grasses help create a haunting scene.

The rubble of the burned church has been cleared away, and only the bell tower remains. A locked fence encloses the church ruins and the cemetery, but visitors can stand nearby and watch and listen. Once in awhile a funeral is held in the cemetery, and families continue to take care of the grounds.

With the telling of the tales, the church came to be known as Old Gunn, its real name and history almost forgotten.

In the darkness of night, with wispy fog obscuring a pale moon or stars, sounds seem ghostly. Visitors listen to bird calls, crackling leaves, possibly caused by footsteps, or the keening of the wind in the high tree limbs. Tombstones gleam in the fading light, as they have for a century and a half. It is a scene ripe for ghosts and hauntings, for those who wait expectantly.

People have found it so, generation after generation.

21

THE DUTCHMAN

OF MEDWAY PLANTATION

The fire smolders and glows in the brick fireplace. The quiet room, lighted only by the fire, fills with flickering shadows as the darkness deepens. It is a special time of day on an old plantation of the South, far removed from the sights and sounds of nearby towns. A lonely solitude settles over the land.

In a heavy wooden armchair near the fire sits a short, stocky gentleman, gazing into the flames. His clothing reflects the styles of the 1600s in Holland or France. He wears a tall, broad-rimmed hat, set with a silver buckle on its band. His jacket, fashioned of rich material, features a wide, snug collar and cuffs. Knee-length pants, stockings and polished buckled shoes complete his outfit.

A heavy, ornate cloak has been thrown over the back of the chair, in the heat of the room. Firelight flickers over the soft green of his clothing and reflects in his silver buttons and buckles. In his hands, he cups a cherished pipe. His bearded face shows a complacent satisfaction with his surroundings.

As the door opens, the gentleman looks around, then slowly vanishes. The fire flickers and the chair remains in place, but he is no longer there. Sometimes a person sleeping in this upstairs bedroom, on the south side of the Manor House of Medway Plantation, may awaken to catch a glimpse of the man, enjoying his pipe before the fire.

His name was Jan Van Arrsens, Seigneur de Weirnhoudt. He built his beloved home, Medway, in 1686 for his beautiful wife, Sabina de Vignon. The young couple had come from Holland to this strange new land of America. Van Arrsens secured a land grant to acreage on the Back River, near Goose Creek, and set about building and landscaping his home.

For more than three centuries, the house has remained on a slight rise above green lawns and plantings, sheltered by huge moss-draped oaks. It faces the Back River, a wide creek which flows into the Cooper River. It is the oldest brick house still standing in South Carolina. Its mellow, rosy bricks were made and dried on the site.

Being a Dutch nobleman, Van Arrsens planned his house to rival those he remembered in Europe. The central section of the structure has "stairstep gables" that encourage evil spirits to walk down them, instead of invading the house. The bedroom where Van Arrsens sometimes sits is located in this section.

Van Arrsens and his wife had no children. They took pride in their home, its furnishings and landscaped grounds. All too soon, Van Arrsens died and his young wife was left alone. She buried her husband at Medway. Without a permanent marker, the grave cannot be found today.

The widow soon married Landgrave Thomas Smith, and they made their home at Medway. The ghost of Van Arrsens began appearing soon after his death. Apparently his wife's remarriage did not upset him. Perhaps he liked the care taken of his home, and the improvements and additions. Those who felt his presence noticed his air of contentment, as he sat by the fire.

Thomas Smith became governor in 1693, under rule of the Proprietors (or owners) of the colony. Medway and Smith's Charleston home became centers of colonial social life.

Smith died November 16, 1694, at the age of forty-six. His grave at Medway is marked by a heavy slab, unlike Van Arrsen's final resting place. Smith had two sons from a former marriage, who later inherited the property.

The Manor House of Medway Plantation
Courtesy of Mary C. Simms-Oliphant, from The History of South Carolina

Medway Plantation had several different owners during its first two hundred years. Lumbering and rice cultivation brought riches to its owners before the Civil War. Peter Gaillard Stoney bought Medway in 1835, and his family owned it for the next ninety years. They added the west wing, and planted the two avenues of live oaks. The earthquake of 1886 caused the stepped gables to crumble, but the Stoneys had them restored.

By the winter of 1929, the house was an abandoned ruin, overgrown with vines and massive bushes. Hunters sometimes used it for a shelter. It seemed that no one would want to buy it or attempt to restore it.

Gertrude and Sidney Legendre first saw the old plantation in 1929 while visiting friends who lived nearby. They admired the avenues of oaks and the pale pink bricks of the aging manor house. Before they left, they decided to buy Medway, Spring Grove, Pine Grove and other pieces of property totaling 8,600 acres.

The restoration and modernization of Medway made a livable and comfortable home for the Legendre family. Formal gardens and carefully designed terraces and walks complement the buildings. It became a special place for the family and for the state of South Carolina.

The Legendres set up the Medway Environmental Trust to preserve and protect the pine and hardwood forests, a refuge for endangered birds and animals.

It seems that the Dutchman of Medway has much to smile about these days. As he sits in his favorite room, shadows lengthen, the fire flickers, and he smokes his treasured pipe. He must approve of the way his house is taken care of and loved.

It's not a bad way to pass the centuries.

22

THE LIGHTS OF LUCAS BAY

She was little and slender and very pretty. Her brothers had always called her "skinny," even after she became an adult, and she had long ago accepted that. They loved her and they also loved to tease her.

Her name was Letty. She stood on the porch of the old house a little longer, watching the road from Georgetown. It was 1865. Just yesterday word had come that Yankee soldiers were already in the harbor town, swarming ashore from their ships. Since they were headed north on General Sherman's "journey of destruction," everyone thought that Conway would be next. Surely the army would be moving on up the coast.

They had heard so many tales of houses looted and burned, after valuables were taken, of course. The troops spread out through the countryside, and no one felt safe. Someone said that the county records had been sent to Chesterfield, South Carolina, farther inland, for safe keeping. So many rumors and frightening tales!

Letty pulled her thin scarf closer around her shoulders in the growing chill of the early spring afternoon. She turned back into her parents' house which stood near the edge of Lucas Bay. It was one of the mysterious bay-formations near the coast, heavily wooded, covered with swampy wet areas and even small lakes. But it had been Letty's childhood playground and refuge. She and her brothers often ventured beyond the edge of the woods to watch for rabbits and deer.

What could she do? Everyone said the Yankees were coming and she wanted to protect her baby from them. That, she knew she must do. Her baby needed her, the baby that Ralph had never seen. His likeness to her soldier husband was uncanny, the "spittin' image," her granddaddy said. She had held onto that thought through the long war, finding comfort in it. Someday Ralph would be back, his blue eyes happy and excited, his arms warm and loving.

In the spring of 1865 the entire country was tired of the war. The end was inevitable, with the South suffering defeat after defeat. The capture and burning of Atlanta, Georgia marked the beginning of General Sherman's march to Savannah, then across South Carolina to Columbia and on north, with massive destruction along the way.

The news was that sometimes the invading soldiers killed babies or threw them in the nearby Pee Dee River. That must not happen to her baby, Ralph's son. He was such a sweet little fellow, tiny and perfectly formed. She held him close and rocked him gently, thinking of her plans. She must work quickly.

Cowford Creek ran across Lucas Bay Swamp and on south into Bull Creek. To the north, a narrow creek, which was often dry, flowed into Cowford. A bridge, hardly more than a footbridge, crossed the flow of water. Letty knew of a cave in the creek's bank. It was only a hollowed out space, but Letty had thought of it as her cave since childhood. Her baby would be safe there.

Lovingly, Letty fed her baby and held him close until he was sound asleep. She talked to him and cuddled him, explaining that his sweet daddy would soon be home to take care of them. As she talked, she laid the baby on pillows in the clothes basket, and covered him with blankets. When he was snug and secure, she slipped out of the house and down the trail to the bridge across the creek. Then she pushed the basket into the small protected area that she called her cave.

Letty gently caressed her sleeping child and left him in the safest place she could think of. Surely the Yankee soldiers would not think of looking in her cave for a mite of a baby boy. She finally left him and raced back to the house. Her mother and sisters were trying to hide everything of value before the soldiers came.

So intent were they on their work that Letty had not noticed the darkening sky. Then she realized that a storm had come up, with strong winds and fierce thunder and lightening. Letty gasped. Her baby would awaken and be frightened by the noise and the rain.

The young mother grabbed a lantern and raced out of the house to the creek and little cave. As she feared, the water was rising up to the basket, and the baby was stirring restlessly. Without regard for herself, Letty rushed across the narrow bridge to reach her baby. Instead she slipped and fell. Her head struck a heavy timber. It knocked Letty unconscious, and she fell into the water. The current kept rising and swept her to the main stream of Cowford Creek and on toward the river. Soon the water dislodged the baby's basket, and it followed her.

*   *   *

What a tragedy for Letty's family and the community. The young mother's body was never found; it was probably swept down river and out to sea. Does Letty still look for her lost baby?

Soon after these tragic events, a mysterious light began to hover over the bridge and wooded thickets, and along the unpaved road. It may be a small, dim light, or a larger lantern, swinging along the road just as a worried mother would carry it–searching, always searching for her precious child.

Numerous accounts of sightings have been recorded. Some residents have seen the light all their lives; others declare that they have never caught a glimpse of it. Rainy, foggy nights are the most likely time to see the Lucas Bay Light. The Civil War ended in 1865, so Letty and her child lost their lives well over a century ago.

The war and the Reconstruction period that followed were times of suffering and grief. Many tragic events occurred. Over the years this story of Letty and her lost child has been repeated uncounted times. No houses sit along the unpaved road beside Lucas Bay. No one walks the road at night, or tarries during the day. It is an eerie place to visit, a place of harsh memories, and feelings that are never fully explained.

23

THE GHOST OF LITCHFIELD MANOR

The sound of the bell ringing at the Litchfield Plantation gate meant that someone wished to be admitted. But strangely enough, there was no one there. To those who heard it, night after night, it had an ominous sound. The eerie ringing continued for years, until new owners finally had the bell removed.

*   *   *

The wrought iron gates, set in old brick walls, open upon a quarter-mile avenue leading to the beautiful manor house of Litchfield Plantation. Giant live oaks, draped with silvery streamers of moss, spread their limbs overhead to create a dusky corridor. Brilliant azaleas, blooming in season, brighten and enhance the beauty of the drive to the picturesque house.

Litchfield Plantation, once the center of a rich "Rice Kingdom," lies along the Waccamaw River, west of the King's Highway. The Simons family, from Litchfield, England, settled on a two-thousand-acre land grant in the early 1700s. The house is estimated to have been built in 1740. In modern times the gracious ante-bellum home has been refurbished and restored to the elegance of more romantic days.

When Peter Simons died in 1794, his sons, Peter and John, inherited the estate. They divided it, with Peter taking the southern

The entrance gate to Litchfield Plantation
Courtesy of J. K. Floyd

half, called Willbrook Plantation. John kept the Litchfield part, including the house. He promptly sold it to the Tuckers of Georgetown, newly arrived from Bermuda.

The Tuckers developed a fine system of flooding and draining their rice fields. As a result, Litchfield Plantation produced one million pounds of rice per year by 1850. The present landing dock on the creek, back of the house, was built in the mid-1800s. Rice freighters sailed up the Waccamaw to the landing to carry rich cargoes to European markets. The Tuckers and other rice planters amassed great fortunes.

John Tucker married three times and fathered nine children, but the estate was not divided when he died. He left it to his third wife's son, Henry Massingberd Tucker. Henry, born in 1831, had trained as a doctor to meet the needs of his large family and great number of slaves. He served with the Confederate army in the Civil War, until the surrender at Appomattox.

At war's end, Henry returned home. He was determined to keep his beloved plantation. He also resolved to serve his family, friends, former slaves and community in every way possible. Many of his freed slaves stayed to live and work in the only place they knew, a place they called home.

Although his medical training was primarily for those in his Rice Kingdom, the good doctor could not turn anyone down. He was the closest doctor to all of the great plantations of Waccamaw Neck. He found many emergencies to treat: accidents, strokes, heart attacks or severe illnesses. Most of the people he treated had no money to offer him, which made no difference. His consideration for those who needed help was well-known.

Often the doctor got called out at night to treat someone who was critically ill. The plantation gate was closed, locked and barred securely behind him as he rode out on his great bay horse, with his saddle bags bulging with medical supplies. An old servant lived alone in a small cabin nearby. He served as gatekeeper.

Returning from a call, the doctor would ride up to the bell. A light tap usually brought the servant to the gate, but if he delayed, the good doctor, cold and tired and growing more frustrated by the minute, would bang on the bell with his silver riding crop.

Unknown to the doctor, the old gatekeeper had fancied a young woman on an adjoining plantation and married her. Often he would slip away to visit her, and not be there to open the gate. As the doctor waited, he would rap the bell so loudly that someone else would come to let him in. Or he would tie his horse, climb the wall, and walk down the long avenue to his home. He used a small staircase in the back of the house to reach his room without disturbing the family.

Dr. Tucker died in 1904; he was buried in Georgetown. The day of great rice fortunes had ended, and the doctor was the last member of the Tucker clan to own the beautiful estate. Some say he never left. Perhaps he loved his Rice Kingdom so much that his spirit remained there after his death.

It was on a foggy, rainy night shortly after the the doctor died that the gatehouse bell began to ring—with no one there. From then on, the eerie sound could be heard from time to time. It came late at night, as if Dr. Tucker had been out on a late call. Successive owners of the plantation heard the ringing, until finally the bell was removed.

Residents of the house have caught a glimpse of a white-haired old gentleman, slowly climbing the back stairs to the bedroom the doctor used. Whenever someone approached, the figure vanished.

Reportedly a horse and rider have been spotted moving along King's Road, and lingering near the Litchfield gate. It happens on dark, foggy nights, when moisture drips from trees laden with the silvery gray moss. If you hear the faint tinkle of a bell borne on a breeze, it might be the good doctor.

Litchfield Plantation is such a beautiful and pleasant place to live, who could blame him for not wanting to leave?

And so the legend lives on.

24

HOMESTEADERS ON
THE DUNES GOLF COURSE

Was it another ghost town settlement? Often small villages flourished for a time and then vanished, leaving few distinguishing landmarks. As a rule, some names were listed or remembered by people living close by. There must have been some interaction with others, but no one found any records.

Clouds of mystery shroud this "happening" in Grand Strand lore. No one seemed to know of the settlement's existence or notice its untimely disappearance, not even travelers along the King's Highway.

During Reconstruction, following the Civil War, the loss of voting rights and paying high taxes caused many people to seek new homes and jobs. The Homestead Act, passed by the United States Congress in 1862, made it possible to claim unsettled land as a homesteader. New settlers were required to file a claim to the land, build a house, make improvements, and live on the property five years. The settlers who had disappeared from the Grand Strand left after a year, so they did not "prove their claim," as it was called.

Losing the family farm and home worked a hardship on many people in the 1870s and 1880s. This was the case with a group of families who lived beyond Lake Waccamaw, in North Carolina.

They decided to follow the Waccamaw River into South Carolina and turn toward the coast. Surely they would find unsettled land to claim as homesteaders, instead of having to buy acreage.

As they discussed their plight, they realized they had little to lose in North Carolina. Some of them had nowhere to go, and were camping on a friend's farm. The word was that Horry County was almost like the western frontier, with unsettled land for the taking. So they packed up, "lock, stock, and barrel," and headed southeast.

Oftentimes history is recorded in bits and pieces picked up from various sources. One report of the passing of the "Waccamaw group" was written by a Myrtle Beach High School student in the 1950s. The student interviewed a very old man who reportedly remembered the coming of the settlers. He said the farmer-pioneers got permission to spend a night on his father's farm. They made camp in a large field and built their campfire in the big circle of wagons. After settling in and preparing some food, they began to sing and dance around the fire.

The old man told the student that, although at the time he was a very young child, he and his family watched the group for a long time. He said neither of his parents had ever seen ordinary people sing and dance like that. Who were the travelers? Did he see a jug? Were they gypsies?

Late that night, smoldering remains of the fire still burned. A soft breeze scattered leaves and pine straw. Rag-tags of fog and cloud traced across the moon, as the people slept in their wagons. The old man had never forgotten that night. He was sorry that he never saw the wagons or people again. His father heard that the group moved on closer to Singleton's Swash and settled there briefly.

At first the area must have seemed like a perfect place to live. The swash and beach offered fish and all kinds of seafood. Also the remnants of a shattered salt works from Civil War days made it easy to obtain salt. Surely they would be able to grow the subsistence crops that farmers depended on.

The men selected a site and set to work building small cabins or houses. Surprisingly, these cabins had block foundations, built from the plentiful coquina rock found along the coast. The homesteaders cut trees to build the cabins, providing shelters for all the families as soon as possible.

To help, the women began to dig and plant food crops among the tree stumps, with little success. It was a typical scene from pioneer days. The water they found tasted bitter or brackish (salty). Swarms of mosquitoes attacked everyone, infecting them with malaria and yellow fever.

The homesteaders probably held on as long as they could. In the fall, coastal storms and hurricanes often swept the area. It was a grim end to their dreams of a prosperous new home.

Abandoning their hopes and dreams, the survivors returned to North Carolina in less than a year, without proving their claims.

Workers discovered the remains of small houses, set in rows, during the construction of the Dunes Golf Course. Remains of the houses had been swept away by the "Great Storm" in August 1893 and the tidal wave that followed in October, but the block foundations were still there. Few people were knowledgeable about the settlement and considered the findings a great mystery.

25

FATEFUL VOYAGE

OF THE FREEDA A. WYLEY

On the beach at 43rd Avenue North in Myrtle Beach lies the burned hulk of an old shipwreck. Often it is entirely covered with heavy sand, but storms with rain and lashing winds uncover it from time to time. It is the only shipwreck remains on this part of the coast. The *Freeda A. Wyley* is a relic of the "Great Storm" of August 28, 1893.

The sailing vessel, a 507-ton barkentine, was carrying a load of heart pine lumber from Pascagoula, Mississippi to New York City. Her home port was Thomaston, Maine. She was on a regular run to the Gulf Coast to transport pine lumber as land was cleared for planting.

The storm left grim statistics behind: seventy ships sunk along the Carolina coast, two thousand people killed, and twenty thousand left homeless. It was a "Killer Hurricane."

If a disabled ship came in along the shore, people quickly gathered to cart away anything usable. Because the *Freeda A. Wyley* had burned, some of it was left to tell the tale.

Sometimes a special agent was put on a ship that was suspected of smuggling to avoid import taxes. Smuggling was a problem from the early days of colonial settlements.

The story that follows was told by a special agent from the Port Authority of Savannah, Georgia:

*   *   *

There it lay, the burned hulk of a splendid ship, anchored in the shifting sands close by the line of dunes. I knew that the old three-masted barkentine had burned to the waterline in a devastating hurricane that struck the Carolinas in August 1893. The ship had finally drifted ashore somewhere along the coast.

It had been two long years since I had seen the ship, called the *Freeda A. Wyley.* Perhaps being here would help the nightmares that had plagued me since that terrible night of the storm. My wife Martha had often insisted that I come here, and she had helped me plan my journey.

I had traveled by train to Wilmington, North Carolina from Savannah, Georgia. There I had hired a horse to bring me to this desolate strip of coast. It lay some miles south of the little fishing village of Little River, South Carolina.

As I made my way down the coast, I talked with people and enjoyed the simple hospitality of fisher-folk. Again and again, they told me of the seventy or more ships and crews that perished in that unforgettable hurricane. They called it "The Great Storm." I learned that the ship's log from the *Freeda A. Wyley* had washed ashore near Shallotte Point, North Carolina.

"Aye, John," one old man told me, "the worst one was the ship that burned. No chance for the poor devils aboard the *Freeda A. Wyley.* You can see what's left of it, down the coast a bit. No one could survive the fire and the storm!"

But I had survived.

Fearfully, I seated myself on a solid beam of the burned wreck. I trembled as my nightmare began, only this time I was awake.

In 1893, my work with the Customs Office in Savannah, Georgia, often involved looking for evidence of smuggling. From time to time, I would pose as an ordinary seaman, picking up bits and pieces of information from the crew of some ship. Smuggling was a fact of life, and every ship sailing the Gulf or Caribbean was suspect. Anything I could learn around the waterfront or on board a ship might help.

The *Freeda A. Wyley* had made a brief stop in the port of Savannah for fresh water and supplies. My superiors learned that a sick sailor was being left behind, so they planned for me to take his place. This

"Fearfully I seated myself on a solid beam of the burned wreck."
Courtesy of J. K. Floyd

ship, bound for New York, had sailed from Pascagoula, Mississippi, with a cargo of virgin yellow pine.

Members of the crew were already weary with the long voyage. They paid little attention to a slender young man, dressed in shabby seaman's garb, and not very skilled in the rigorous art of sailing.

I soon realized that Al and Jake were the bosses of the crew. I tried to stay out of their way, but I watched and listened. In fact, I said little to anyone. I simply tried to do my job as well as I could.

The ship was in heavy seas from the moment we sailed out of the mouth of the Savannah River. The weather was cloudy and hot and the sky was completely overcast, with threatening banks of clouds. On August 28, the storm worsened, with gale-force winds blowing sheets of rain. By nightfall, we knew we were in trouble.

I figured the captain would have to remain on the bridge and all the sailors at their posts. In spite of the rough seas, it might be my only opportunity to look for evidence of smuggling. Making sure no one saw me, I slipped into the captain's cabin.

I had lit the lantern and shielded its dim glow to examine the ship's log when I suddenly felt myself seized by both shoulders.

"Snoopin', eh?" a harsh voice grunted. "Wanta show him what happens to snoopers?" Turning my head, I had a glimpse of Al and Jake and their leering faces.

"Stickin' his nose where he's got no business," one of them chortled. "Maybe a swim will teach him!"

The horror of that moment returns to me. My swimming skills were even poorer than my seamanship. Anyway, who could swim in such a sea? My cries and struggles only amused the two men. They picked me up easily, held me suspended over the rail, and threw me into that boiling whirling sea, surely to my death.

I will never know how I made it to land. Later, it occurred to me that I had literally been flung ashore by the giant surging waves of the rising tide. I know now that the ship had been following the coastline as closely as possible. Its location was just off Frying Pan Shoals, near the mouth of the Cape Fear River.

So, miraculously, I was still alive.

For long minutes I lay there gasping, unable to move, barely conscious. Cold rain on my shoulders and sand in my mouth alerted me to my predicament. I began to hitch myself along the beach in a kind of crawl until I was out of the water. Every part of my body was in pain as I struggled and worked my way to the dunes.

When I could raise myself a bit, I stared in every direction. I could see no sign of the ship in the inky darkness of the night. The waves were mountainous, rolling and heaving, lashed by the fierce thrust of the wind.

Stumbling, half-crawling, blown down by the wind, I made my way farther back from the beach. Instinctively, I knew I had to find some kind of shelter. Even a cluster of bushes might help. I finally found a crude open structure, probably used by fishermen. It had partially collapsed, but it offered me some slight protection. I crouched there for a time, my body racked by cold and pain and exhaustion.

I was jolted awake, without realizing I was dozing, by the high keening of the wind. The storm had abated somewhat, although the cold rain still fell in great gusts. My arms and legs were stiff and sore from cuts and bruises, my clothes in tatters, but I was alive! I could scarcely believe the startling events of the night.

The sky was brightening fast beyond the reach of the beach but still black dark behind me. I turned painfully toward the water. I could see that the sky was lit up, but not from the dawn, as I had thought. It was more like the glow of a distant fire, now dim, now bright, shining through the darkness of the storm. I watched with alarm, fearful that my ship, the *Freeda A. Wyley*, was afire.

Pushing myself to my feet, I stumbled and crawled back toward the beach, but water was pouring over the tops of the high dunes. And though I watched and called and cursed my helplessness, I could do nothing for those poor souls aboard the burning ship. Its cargo of pine burned like kindling, in spite of the rain and the sea, as the ship turned and tossed in its death agony.

The sun was hot on my shoulders as I eased myself down to stand for awhile beside the charred remains of the barkentine. Seagulls wheeled above me and sandpipers scurried busily just along the water's edge.

I had come face to face with my nightmare. Perhaps now, God willing, I could cast it aside.

It was time for me to go.

26

BELLE'S HOUSE

BELLEFIELD

She called her new home "Bellefield," and it was a splendid choice. After all, she was Belle Baruch, daughter of Bernard Baruch, whose extensive land holdings on Waccamaw Neck in South Carolina are known to this day as "Hobcaw Barony." One of the old abandoned rice plantations he had acquired was Bellefield, and this was the one Belle wanted to buy in 1936 for her very own home.

Waccamaw Neck is a beautiful and interesting place to visit and explore. It comes complete with tales of Indians who roamed the land for countless centuries, and Spaniards who tried to settle in the 1500s, and failed. Numbers of pirates found refuge in the inlets and coves in the early 1700s, as they preyed on colonial trade. The Neck has seen exciting times, with fierce and dangerous events taking place in war and peace.

Is it any wonder that spirits of bygone days linger?

Belle's father, Bernard Baruch, was a Wall Street millionaire and financier at age thirty. This "Wizard of Wall Street," as he was called, willingly served as an unpaid "Advisor to Presidents." Beginning with President Woodrow Wilson in World War I, he served five presidents through World War II. Wilson nicknamed him "Dr.

Facts." Others called him "The Park Bench Statesman," since he didn't work out of an office.

Bernard Baruch was born in Camden, South Carolina in 1870. His father, who had been a Confederate surgeon in the Civil War, decided to move his family to New York City in 1880. There young Baruch grew up and graduated from City College, but he never forgot his early boyhood days in South Carolina. He dreamed of warm sunny weather, of streams for fishing and woods for hunting.

In 1905 Baruch discovered Waccamaw Neck while on a hunting trip. Within two years, he had bought eleven of the thirteen plantations on the Neck. He had found a place of rest and relaxation for himself and his family.

The family chose Friendship House on Winyah Bay, a remodeled manor house on one of the plantations, for their winter home.

Hobcaw Barony was a wilderness estate of 17,500 acres, deserted except for a few slave family descendants who had remained in one of the old slave villages. Hobcaw was Belle's favorite place in the world, although they had a Park Avenue apartment in New York and spent summers in Europe. At Hobcaw, she led her brother and sister into all sorts of escapades. She loved to hunt and fish and roam through the woods with the dogs. When time came to return to New York, Belle always wanted to stay at Hobcaw.

Friendship House burned at Christmas in 1929. The Baruchs built a second home of brick, as fireproof as possible. By 1931 Hobcaw House stood proudly on a bluff overlooking Winyah Bay, with a view of Georgetown across the water. The rosy brick house, with its white columns, was surrounded by moss-draped oaks hovering over colorful azaleas, camellias, hollies and dogwood.

Baruch called his nine-bedroom mansion his "hunting lodge." It had every luxury except a telephone, which he considered just a nuisance. The servants' wing on the back had eight more bedrooms.

Baruch also bought and developed property on the Black River, between Nesmith and Kingstree, South Carolina. He called his house there "Little Hobcaw." He and his wife Annie enjoyed spending winters in the smaller house. Mrs. Baruch died in 1938. The Baruchs had entertained many of the world's famous people in both homes. Great leaders valued Baruch's advice.

From her first sight of Waccamaw Neck, Belle loved it. As she grew up she felt a deep desire and commitment to preserve Hobcaw Barony, to keep it in its natural state. In 1936 she bought Bellefield from her father and built her home there. As time went by, she bought all of Hobcaw Barony, and made plans to take care of it.

Bellefield Plantation had no manor house when Belle bought it. Mysteriously, the house, built in the early 1800s, had burned before it was ever lived in. She heard this tale and many more. She was also told that none of the local workers went there willingly. Belle was well-pleased with the lay of the land and its location on Winyah Bay. She would have plenty of room for her horses and stables and her other animals. She could also build a runway for her small plane.

Besides, the plantation had her name, and she knew in her heart that it would be her home. She built her home on a low bluff overlooking Winyah Bay. It had been the exact location of the first manor house.

Belle had many projects in mind for the estate. She wanted to improve the housing of the workers and schools for the children. She knew that better medical care was needed. Belle set up a foundation to fund research that would help preserve the coastal region. She had many interests and lived a happy, productive life, until her untimely death in 1964 from cancer. Her life at Bellefield was the fulfillment of her dream.

*   *   *

But what of the house that burned so mysteriously? Why did no one ever live in the lovely structure?

The owner of Bellefield in the early 1800s was a handsome young man named Thomas Young. His story was the classic scenario of a poor young man falling in love with the beautiful, sheltered daughter of a wealthy rice planter. It happened often in the South, where men were measured by their land and wealth instead of by their worthy characteristics.

Despite the difference in their social status, the young couple married. Young had inherited rich, uncleared land on Waccamaw Neck, but he had little money to develop it. It was his fervent dream to clear the land for rice fields and build an elegant home for his lovely bride. So he outlined a tremendous task for himself and the few slaves he was able to purchase. Young himself worked harder than any slave. He was out in the fields before dawn, working with the slaves, preparing fields for planting rice, and digging canals for the necessary water supply. He supervised all the details of plantation life.

When it became too dark to work in the fields, exhausted slaves crept away to their cabins, but not Thomas Young. Each night he went at once to the house to check the work done by the carpenters. He could be seen with his lantern, going from room to room, carefully examining the work of the day. He carried a hammer and often stopped to finish some detail begun by the builders.

Young dreamed of the day when he and his wife would entertain wealthy and important people. He wanted visitors to be impressed with the beauty and elegance of his home, and perhaps envy him. His dreams kept him going. His wife scarcely saw him, and when she did he was too preoccupied to talk to her. After working long hours, he sometimes fell asleep in the new house instead of going to their temporary home.

His wife pleaded with him to slow down and rest. Surely this was no way to spend their honeymoon year. He insisted that the house would soon be finished and he could rest then. By day he worked in the fields, and night after night he worked on the house. As his rigorous schedule continued, he lost weight and his health began to fail.

Young's slaves realized how tired and worn he had become. Each night they watched the light of his lantern moving through the house. They knew that long after everyone else was asleep, their master would still be working.

When Young's home was almost completed, he intensified his work, longing to move in and see the faces of admiring visitors, but he finally went beyond the limits of his endurance. One day he collapsed with a seizure. His slaves managed to put him on a horse and take him to his wife. She did everything she could for him, but three days later he died.

It was a sorry day on the Neck. Everyone had seen how hard Young worked, and how determined he had been to complete his dream house. The other planters of Waccamaw Neck came to pay their respects to the young widow.

The manor house was finished, but Thomas Young's wife could not bring herself to move in. She even blamed the lovely house for killing her husband. As time went by, the slaves were sold and the fields lay untended. The house stood empty and abandoned. It soon took on the look of an older building. Young's wife, saddened and lonely, moved away.

Before long, there were stories of unexplained lights appearing in the empty house. The slaves came to watch, remembering how hard Young had worked to finish the house. One runaway slave hid in the house and went to sleep. He awakened later and saw a light moving up the stairs. When he forced himself to look closely, he saw a figure with a lantern and a hammer, the figure of Thomas Young. The story spread quickly through the plantations.

From time to time, boaters on Winyah Bay mentioned seeing lights in Bellefield House, where no one lived. Always they mentioned the light of a lantern, moving from room to room.

Sightings of Young's lantern continued over the years, as the house grew old and deteriorated. Finally one night it burned to the ground, with nothing left but the foundation.

*   *   *

Belle Baruch's beautiful home at Bellefield was often filled with guests, who enjoyed the Neck as much as she did. Many of her visitors were well-known, coming from Washington, D.C., Hollywood, Australia and Europe. In 1944 President Franklin D. Roosevelt spent almost a month at Hobcaw House, as a guest of Belle's father. He came for rest and relaxation, as his health was failing. On several occasions he was taken to Bellefield to visit and talk with Belle. He enjoyed her sharp wit and remarks. She always made him laugh.

Perhaps Thomas Young's dream finally came true after all—a beautiful manor house on the bluff above Winyah Bay, with honored guests arriving and enjoying their visits. They say that Young's lantern has not been seen for many years.

Maybe his restless spirit is at last at peace.

27

ATALAYA

"CASTLE IN THE SAND"

Atalaya was his Spanish "Castle in the Sand."

Archer Milton Huntington, philanthropist and founder of Brookgreen Gardens in 1931, had traveled in Europe as a child with his parents. He saw and admired Moorish fortresses on the southeastern coast of Spain. They were built with low sturdy walls to withstand the lashing attacks of Atlantic storms. He and his wife, Anna Hyatt Huntington, adapted the plan and design for a winter home on the sometimes stormy coast of South Carolina.

Since the early 1930s, the Huntingtons' "castle" has stood among palm trees, myrtles and pines, firmly anchored in deep sand. It is located in Huntington State Park, known from colonial days as Magnolia Beach.

The 2,500-acre park lies about three miles south of Murrells Inlet, and across from Brookgreen Gardens. A private estate until Huntington's death in 1955, it became a state park in 1960. For years it has served as the setting for numerous arts and crafts shows. The park is also a natural habitat for saltwater and fresh water wildlife, alligators and birds, with boardwalks for viewers.

In 1930 the Huntingtons bought four adjoining plantations located on Waccamaw Neck. The land stretched from the Waccamaw

River to the sandy beach of the Atlantic Ocean. They planned outdoor statuary gardens to display the work of Mrs. Huntington and numerous other sculptors. Although they had several other homes, they built Atalaya between 1930-1933 as a winter home.

Huntington had inherited a great fortune, but he realized that many thousands of Americans in those years of the Great Depression were jobless, homeless, hopeless, and destitute. He hired as many local people as he could to work in the gardens and on his home. He offered on-the-job training to local brick masons, their helpers, carpenters, painters, all kinds of craftsmen, gardeners and landscapers. What a tremendous gift to the people of the Neck!

Atalaya, "The Spanish Fortress Castle," nestles low in the sand. The building, including the curving walls, the archway, and the patterned floor, is built entirely of brick. Each side of the quadrangle measures two hundred feet. The rooms and passage on each side surround a large open courtyard with covered walkways leading to a forty-foot central tower. There are steps to the front roof, a lookout location, and to underground storage rooms.

The castle was heated entirely by open fireplaces. The thirty-six rooms contain twenty-two fireplaces. Huntington wanted to give the brick masons plenty of work, and he wanted a fireproof home.

He used steel beams through the outer walls to protect against earthquakes or hurricanes. The castle has survived two major storms and many other "hard blows." He also built a spacious studio for Mrs. Huntington with a twenty-five-foot ceiling and skylight, and stables close by for animal models.

Atalaya is open to the public for the art shows, for viewing the castle, and for a scary night show at Halloween. It's a boyhood dream come true—Archer Huntington's "Spanish Castle in the Sand."

Even viewed from afar, Atalaya has a haunted look. It seems to be waiting for ghostly events from the past, for long-gone persons who traveled the coast and stopped along beautiful Huntington Beach. There are those who believe that Theodosia's presence hovers over Magnolia Beach. She often escaped the heat and humidity of her plantation home at The Oaks for the coolness of the beach. If she was lost at sea, perhaps she tries to come back to her beloved husband and son.

Atalaya seems more haunted than ever during the month of October. Special tours are held for "Haunted Halloween at Atalaya." From far and wide come families for a scary treat. The Moorish-style castle is filled with all sorts of ghouls, goblins, ghostly apparitions, and other-world creatures. Even bloody pirates, including Black-beard, sometimes appear to add to the visitors' fun.

Built to withstand storms and earthquakes, Atalaya seems inde-structible, a vacant castle in the sand, perhaps inhabited by the spirits of those who have gone on before.

The lookout tower in the central court of Atalaya
Courtesy of J. K. Floyd

28

RESIDENT GHOSTS

At one time, Georgetown County claims to have had 162 plantations, each with a registered name. Each name had a story behind it, and it also helped locate the property. Of the great rice and indigo plantations in pre-Civil War days, at least one hundred claimed resident ghosts. No one argued or asked too many questions about these presences. They were simply accepted as part of the tales or folklore that made up the rich heritage of the coastal lands. It was your privilege to believe or not.

The manifestations of ghosts take many forms. In two instances, frisky little terriers run and play together, inviting onlookers to join the fun. However, if anyone comes too close or tries to touch them, they immediately vanish. Two terriers can be seen from time to time at Pawleys Island and two at Medway Plantation at Goose Creek, near Charleston. You may hear faint cries of the little boy whose hand was caught as he reached down into a hole to catch a crab. Instead the tide came in and caught him.

In 1764 Thomas and Mary Allston married and built a manor house, Prospect Hill, on their 550-acre plantation. He died in 1794, and Mary, his childless widow, turned her attention and her devotion to managing the plantation and taking care of the five hundred slaves.

She knew most of them by name, and they returned her love multi-fold.

In a few years, Mary married Benjamin Huger, Jr. He died in 1823. Again she found consolation in caring for her slaves and the plantation. When she became ill, she had to stay in her bedroom and on the small portico near her room. The slaves often sat below her room at night, watching her light and singing the melodious spirituals that she loved so much.

After her death, the slaves continued to gather beneath the portico and sadly sing songs. Their tears flowed as they realized their beloved "Miss Mary" was gone. And then one night they saw a tiny light in her room. As they waited in breathless delight, they saw Miss Mary's figure outlined in a glow of light on the portico. To them it meant that their dear mistress was still looking after them.

It seems that every nook and cranny in Georgetown County has its own special story, repeated many times, whether it involves lights or sounds or appearances. Or it may be just a feeling of a presence, unseen and unheard.

The Rhem House is located across the Georgetown-Williamsburg county line, on Highway S.C. 51. Sharon Owens rented the house, although she had been told that it was haunted. She informed everyone that she didn't believe in ghosts, and she needed a place to live. She stayed in the house about a year, and often felt a presence; someone, unseen, was in the room with her. It was a strange feeling for Sharon, but not really a scary one.

Jim McLendon is the current owner of Rhem House. He says the house was built in 1890 for the Rhem family. They owned a lot of land and most of it was forested; they harvested turpentine from the tall pines. It was a lucrative business, as long as most ships were wooden.

McLendon says Mrs. Rhem is the legendary ghost, the "Keeper of the House," the spirit from earlier days. She loved music, and pianos and stereos have been known to play suddenly, with no one there. He also reported catching a glimpse of a tall lady in a long white dress passing his bedroom door.

Others who have lived there have described the same phenomena, a feeling of a presence, seldom glimpsed by anyone. It is not a frightening experience. Neither is it a reassuring one. Perhaps the lady is simply looking after her house, as the lady of any house did, with the help of her slaves.

Many of the great old plantations have passed on to other owners, complete with their legends and tales, some of their furnishings, and many times, their ghosts. Where else would the resident spirits go?

Once again, the past merges with the present, in an area where "ghosting" is commonplace and, to many, a way of life. The sightings, whether real, imagined, or contrived, have filled many books over the years. Organized ghost walks and special tours keep the stories alive and the interest level high.

Charleston has a year-round ghost tour, founded in 1994. It includes some of the South's eeriest tales, complete with Gullah language and superstitions. In the city, haunted inns, theaters, graveyards and town houses furnish many more tales.

Georgetown, South Carolina's third oldest city, is steeped in the lore that settlers brought with them from "the Old Country." Family names and stories reflect a rich heritage from England, Ireland, Scotland, France, Germany, and Africa. It's a colorful mixture, along with Indian legends and seafaring lore.

Many times, a person dies with a problem of unfinished business on his mind. Perhaps his restless spirit strives to become reconciled to past events.

It seems that there is no exact science of ghosting, although some people make a career of delving into the supernatural. Rather, it is a gathering of thought, a recording of incidents, and an exploring of possibilities, in an attempt to reach a conclusion.

Fear of the unknown is always a factor coloring the viewpoint of observers. An example might be workers along Plantersville Road, where Old Gunn Church is located. As the shadows of night come with sunset, workers slip away from the job. They refuse to go past the old church after dark. Whether they see anything or not, the possibility is always there, lurking in their minds.

Each generation finds its own version of the science of ghosting, to explore and enjoy.

29

A VOICE FROM THE GRAVE

Tim was sixteen, but little and scrawny, and tense as a startled bird. His long thin legs carried him along that night, and his feet beat a tattoo on the narrow road as he ran.

He knew he was late. He also knew his Pa was wide awake, waiting for him to creep shamefaced into the farm house. Ma would be there too, not saying much but hoping he would come soon. When Pa started, no one could get a word in. They just had to wait until the tongue-lashing ended. Except when it ended, Pa walked away and would not listen.

Mostly Tim hated it for his Ma, because it hurt her. He was used to Pa's tongue-lashings. It seemed like he couldn't do anything to please Pa these days.

Tim was increasingly anxious to be with other young people. He had begged to go to the ballgame, and promised to come straight home afterwards. He didn't mind the two-mile walk to the school. It was great to sit with friends and cheer for the team. Afterwards, instead of going home, he drifted with the crowd to the corner store, and they shared cokes and goofed off.

Before Tim realized it, the time was nearly eleven. He was already late and in trouble, but he would try to get home as soon as possible.

The night was so dark that Tim could scarcely see anything as he ran. A few stars kept appearing and a thin crescent of moon peeped out as clouds floated by. He kept on running, his breath coming in gasps.

Suddenly the wrought iron gate of the local cemetery appeared before him, and he slowed his pace. He could save time by going through the cemetery. Why not try it?

Tim swung the heavy gate open just enough to slip through and ran on, dodging tombstones. There was so little light he could hardly find his way, but he galloped as fast as he could go.

All at once he missed a step and then another. He knew he was falling, clutching at empty air. What had happened? He landed in the bottom of an empty, newly-dug grave, his face in the damp earth. He pushed himself to his feet and brushed dirt from his face. It had been dark before, but nothing like this.

He desperately tried to climb up the sides of the grave. Everywhere he dug in his fingers, the dirt gave way. Then he began to yell for someone, anyone, to help him.

Tim yelled until he was hoarse, and then sank down on the damp, crumbly soil. He began to moan and call out that he was cold. Finally he heard steps, stumbling, meandering across the graveyard. A voice mumbled and sang off key. It was the town drunk. What was he doing out here? Tim raised himself up and called, "I'm cold! Please help me!"

When he heard the slow steps come near the grave, Tim shouted with all his might, sure he would be helped. Instead he heard the gravelly voice of the drunk man: "Ho, ho! Look at you! Of course you're cold. You've kicked your covers off." The heavy steps plodded on, as the drunk man went on his way, singing and bumping into tombstones. Tim sank down helplessly, weeping in his disappointment.

He must have slept, cold and damp as he was. He roused to find himself curled into a ball, trying to keep warm. The stars and thin sliver of moon were covered with clouds and fog. A light sprinkle of rain fell on Tim's upturned face, as he hopelessly settled down again. All he could pray for now was that they wouldn't bury someone else on top of him. Briefly he wondered whose grave he was lying in. Then he thought of his Pa waiting for him. Oh, what could he do?

Gradually Tim calmed down and lay half asleep, in spite of the light rain. He did not hear the footsteps hurrying along, but suddenly he felt a jolt, as a heavy object fell into the grave. He kept quiet at first, not sure whether it was a man or an animal. Someone started clawing at the wall of earth and trying to climb up, but the dirt gave way. It was another boy, and he began yelling as he realized his plight. Tim recognized the voice of a classmate named Jack.

Tim waited a moment before he spoke. Then he said slowly, his voice hoarse from yelling, "It's no use. You'll never get out of here. Don't even try."

Jack hesitated a moment. Then he literally rose up in the air, grappling the wall of earth, until he could grasp a tuft of grass on top. He struggled, terror-filled, until he pulled himself out of the grave. Away he went, running faster than he had ever run before. In the darkness he did not see Tim.

Following Jack's example, Tim was able to climb out of his grave-prison and make his way home. He received the welcome from his Pa that he expected. When he made no reply or excuse, his Pa looked at him and noticed the dirt on his clothes and shoes.

"What happened to you? Did you get into a fight?"

"No," Tim replied, "I fell into a hole."

At school the next day, Jack told everyone what had happened to him. He said he fell into a grave and a ghost threatened him. After school, he took a bunch of his cronies to the cemetery to prove his tale. Tim followed along, listening as Jack enlarged on his story. Tim never said a word. In a way, it was more fun for everybody to believe in the ghost story.

Later on, Tim confided to his Ma, and they laughed together. Jack continued to tell his story and became a hero of sorts. Tim listened with a twinkle in his eye and a secret smile on his face. Jack's story of the voice from the grave became a local legend.